'The mark of a civilised society is how it treats its most vulnerable members.'

Neil Carpenter

Austerity's Victims

Adults with a Learning Disability

ISBN-13: 978-1984977601

ISBN-10: 1984977601

Acknowledgements

In producing this book, there are many people to whom I am grateful.

Thanks go to Lauren Bayfield and Sue Wright for their suggestions, Philip Kennedy for his imagination in designing the cover, Scott Newland for his relaxed precision in formatting the book and Mark Burch for meticulously checking my use of statistics. Any errors that remain are my responsibility, not his.

For their consistent help, I am also indebted to staff working for Mencap and at Cornish day centres. A special thankyou to Gordon Christie who, as a fellow volunteer for an advocacy organisation, has been a constant source of support and advice.

Above all, thanks to the people on whom my case studies focus.

March 2018

Contents

Who are they?

We live in times dominated by the word 'austerity'. National news channels debate Budget figures and cuts in billions. Local news media have that same debate – but only in millions. The people at the bottom of society glimpse a vanishing £10 or £20 and fear what its impact will be on their lives.

But who are those people at the bottom? For many, they are 'scroungers', turning down work to live on benefits that others have paid for and a different species from 'the hardworking families' that certain politicians love to praise.

Look more closely and the stereotype disintegrates. There will always, inevitably, be some 'scroungers' but dwarfing their numbers are families using food banks, men and women with two or three part-time jobs, perhaps on zero hours contracts, as well as individuals with a physical disability – and, of course, many to whom more than one of those descriptions apply.

Buried in those numbers at the bottom are adults with a learning disability. They barely rate a mention, even in publications that are sympathetic to the disadvantaged, and yet People with Learning Disabilities in England 2015[1] estimated that in the country as a whole there were 930,400 adults aged 18+ with a learning disability. In Cornwall, from where the examples in the chapters below are drawn, in 2014-15 there were 940 adults (18 to 64) with a learning disability getting long term support from the Local Authority, according to the Learning Disabilities Health Profile 2015[2]. The same report set the figure at 2,872 'people (all ages) with a learning disability known to GPs'.[3]

The aim of this book is to shine a light on those Cornish adults – their finances and their quality of life. Comparing their circumstances with current norms in Cornwall and in the UK should make it more difficult for those adults and others across the country to be lost, not just in the debate but in their local communities.

Economic and Political Background – 2010-2018

In 2010, the Conservatives and Liberal Democrats formed a coalition government and made it their top declared priority to 'clear up', as they put it on innumerable occasions, 'the financial mess left by Labour'. To achieve this, they embarked on a series of cuts to reduce the deficit. With Health, Education and Overseas Aid spending protected, the axe had to fall elsewhere.

Benefits became an obvious target because of the proportion of the state's spending that they took up. With spending on those of pension age exempt, the scale of the cuts required to working-age benefits increased significantly. Analysis in the Guardian on 22 March 2016, using Department for Work and Pensions (DWP) figures, looked at welfare spending in the 2010-11 Budget and the 2020-21 projected Budget. In 2010-11, pensions and age-related benefits such as the Winter Fuel Payment totalled 43.63% of overall welfare spending; by 2020-21, it was projected that they would total 50.05%. Over this ten year period, because of the growth in spending on those of pension age, working age benefits were bound to suffer.

To justify its measures, the government had to sustain the shift in the electorate's attitudes to working age benefit recipients that according to NatCen Social Research had occurred in the late 1990s and early 2000s.[4] The more it could demonise those who received such benefits as 'scroungers', the more reasonable the programme of cuts would appear.[5]

Senior Conservative politicians, in particular, highlighted what they saw as the injustice of the lifestyle 'enjoyed' by those on working age benefits, most strikingly in George Osborne's 2012 comment:

'Where is the fairness, we ask, for the shift-worker, leaving home in the dark hours of the early morning, who looks up at the closed blinds of their next door neighbour sleeping off a life on benefits?'

Benefit claimants were presented as a deadweight on the country dragging down 'hardworking families who do the right thing'. The contrast was, of course, a false one because many families with one or more adults in employment themselves received benefits but the words 'hardworking families' or 'hardworking people' became a near-constant element in government ministers' speeches – for instance, Grant Shapps, co-chairman of the Conservative Party at the time and the man who in his other persona, Michael Green, sold a marketing product called 'Stinking Rich 3', greeted George Osborne's 2014 Budget with the patronising tweet:

'Cutting the bingo tax and beer duty to help hardworking people to do more of the things they enjoy.'

The press sympathetic to their views emphasised the message. Max Hastings wrote in the Daily Mail on 30 October 2010:

'At last Britain's woken up to the grotesque irony that so many on welfare are better off than hard working families...'

With the victory of the Conservatives at the 2015 election, the framing of David Cameron's policies continued in the same vein. At his first post-election Cabinet meeting, he presented the Tories as 'the real party of working people'. The Queen's Speech on 27 May 2015 opened with these words: 'My government will legislate in the interests of everyone in our country. It will adopt a one nation approach, helping working people get on ...' The impression was egalitarian; the reality was the exclusion of those on working age benefits, for whom a largely unspecified £12bn of welfare cuts promised at the election were imminent.

George Osborne's emergency Budget of 8 July 2015 made the promise specific. The package of measures on benefits, according to the Institute for Fiscal Studies (IFS) analysis[6] on the following day, was 'regressive – taking much more from poorer households than richer ones'. The analysis also concluded that, 'After about 2017 this will mean that most benefit rates will have fallen back behind their 2008 levels both relative to price inflation and relative to earnings growth.' Later in the year, this trend was put in a longer-term context in the IFS analysis[7] of the Autumn Statement of 25 November 2015: 'Benefit spending excluding state pensions in 2020-21 (is) forecast to be at its lowest as a share of national income for thirty years.'

The disabled were among those hit particularly hard by government policy. 'A Fair Society: How The Cuts Target Disabled People'[8] found that 'When we look at the combined impact' (a term that covered cuts in social care, working age benefits and housing as well as regressive tax increases) 'of all the cuts we find ... disabled people (8% of the population) bear 29% of all cuts'. The House of Lords also identified this as a pressing concern for government and recommended that 'The government produce an assessment of the cumulative impact of budgets and other major initiatives on disabled people'.[9]

The sharpest measures affecting the disabled, however, emerged in the Budget of 16 March 2016 which set out plans to cut £1.3 billion a year from Personal Independence Payment (PIP) for people who need aids to help them dress and visit the toilet. The IFS[10] calculated that as a result 370,000 men and women would, on average, lose £3,500 a year.

Reaction in much of the media was critical, especially as the measures could be set against income tax changes in the same Budget which according to analysis by the Resolution Foundation benefited the well-off, 'with over 80% of the gains going to the top half of the income distribution and roughly half (47%) going to the top 20% of households alone'.[11] The momentum behind the criticisms grew after the resignation of Ian Duncan Smith, the Secretary for Work and Pensions, on 18 March and his subsequent comments on the Andrew Marr show on 20 March. Although he had been for almost six years a member of a government implementing cuts to welfare, he voiced his 'deep concern' at a 'very narrow attack on working-age benefits' while at the same time protecting pensioner benefits. He also gave his own explanation for why Tory measures had been focused on the poor: 'It just looks like we see this as a pot of money, that it doesn't matter because they don't vote for us.'

In the face of growing opposition, on 21 March the government announced that the changes to PIP proposed in the Budget were being scrapped. For many, however, the government's true colours had been shown, despite George Osborne, in his opening speech in the Budget debate on 22 March, declaring himself on the side of 'social justice': 'There is not some inherent conflict between delivering social justice and the savings required to deliver sound public finances. They are one and the same thing. Without sound public finances there is no social justice.'

On other occasions, the benefit cuts, to smooth their passage, were given a similar gloss, an 'ethical' dimension. Jeremy Hunt at the Conservative Party Conference in early October 2015 suggested that people dependent on tax credits and benefits lacked self-respect. 'Dignity is not just about how much money you have got ... officially, children are growing up in poverty if there is an income in that family of less than £16,500. What the Conservatives say is how that £16,500 is earned matters.

'It matters if you are earning that yourself, because if you are earning it yourself you are independent and that is the first step towards self-respect. If that £16,500 is either a high proportion or entirely through the benefit system you are trapped. It is about pathways to work, pathways to independence ... It is about creating a pathway to independence, self-respect and dignity.'

His comments, like those of so many politicians, ignored the reality of the people described later in this book for whom paid work may not be possible and for whom independence is only found through benefits and consistent support. At the same time, the words of Hunt and others undermined the 'self-respect and dignity' which in some cases it had taken years to build.

Direct criticism, however, of the disabled by politicians, national or local, was rare[12] – perhaps because of genuine sympathy with their circumstances or perhaps because focus groups and such surveys as NatCen's[13] told them that adverse comment was electorally unpopular. As a result, the term 'benefits' worked for each government from 2010 onwards by being generalised and eased the path for continuing reductions in expenditure.

Whatever people's attitudes to the objectives behind these cutbacks, once they have read the case studies in Chapter 4 onwards, they will be hard-pressed to dispute the effect of the measures set in train in 2010.

Income and Spending across the UK

Before I look, however, at individual adults with a learning disability in Cornwall and how they have been affected by austerity, it's important to establish what the income and standard of living of the 'average' UK citizen are currently.

Across the UK, full-time median gross weekly pay was £539 in April 2016[14]. The median is the mid-point of all wages - an average which does not reveal regional variations, different rates of pay for men and women or the gap between those in full-time employment and those in part-time work and/or on zero hours contracts. It does, nonetheless, provide a national benchmark and converts[15], again as an average, into a net figure of £427 a week.

For Cornwall, full-time median gross weekly pay was £470 in April 2016[16], providing a county benchmark which converts into a net figure of £381 a week.

But how far does that median income go? Analysis published by the Office for National Statistics (ONS)[17] in February 2017 showed average UK weekly household spending was £528.90[18] in the year ending March 2016.

Table 1 - Average UK Weekly Household Spending

Commodity or Service	Average weekly expenditure all households (£)
Food and non-alcoholic drinks	56.80
Alcoholic drinks and tobacco	11.40
Clothing and footwear	23.50
Housing (net[19]), fuel, power and water	72.50
Household goods and services	35.50
Health[20]	7.20
Transport[21]	72.70
Communication (post, telephone etc.)	16.00
Recreation and culture (including TV Licence)	68.00
Education	7.00
Restaurants and hotels (including canteen meals, takeaways, snacks and holidays)	45.10
Miscellaneous goods and services (including hair, toiletries, contents and appliance insurance)	39.70
Other expenditure items (including mortgage interest payments, Council Tax, presents and donations)[22]	73.60

Obviously, the table's breakdown of average weekly expenditure does not reduce consistently for someone on a lower income as some of these areas of expenditure - for example, 'Recreation and culture' – may be less important to the people interviewed later in the book than essentials such as food and heating. Such areas do, nonetheless, serve to highlight what anyone on a much lower income misses out on.

How much lower, however, can income go and still provide an 'adequate' standard of living? Any definition of 'adequacy' is, to some extent, subjective but in a study, 'A Minimum Income Standard for the UK in 2016'[23], researchers priced up what members of the public think people need to achieve a socially acceptable living standard.

The conclusions of the study were that in 2016 single men and women needed to earn £17,100 a year before tax or approximately £329 a week to afford a minimum acceptable standard of living. This converts into a net figure of approximately £285 a week.

This overall total of £285 is included in Table 2 below but without being broken down into spending categories.[24] The other columns of the table adjust the ONS figures in Table 1 (which are for households) into possible spending for a single person on UK full-time median net pay and the Cornwall equivalent.

Table 2 - Comparison of Possible Spending, Living on UK and Cornwall Median Income or on the UK Minimum Income Standard

	Spending on UK full-time, median net pay per week April 2016 (£)[25]	Spending on Cornwall full-time, median net pay per week April 2016 (£)[26]	Spending on UK Minimum Income Standard – net income per week July 2016 (£)
Food and non-alcoholic drinks	29.00[27]	29.00	
Alcoholic drinks and tobacco	24.49	18.36	
Clothing and footwear	8.50	8.50	
Housing (net), fuel, power and water	66.30	66.30	
Household goods and services	19.20	19.20	
Health	3.40	3.40	
Transport	36.20	36.20	
Communication (post, telephone etc.)	10.40	10.40	
Recreation and culture (including TV Licence)	91.48	68.58	
Education	1.10	1.10	
Restaurants and hotels (including canteen meals, takeaways, snacks and holidays/short breaks)	67.83	50.86	

	Spending on UK full-time, median net pay per week April 2016 (£)	Spending on Cornwall full-time, median net pay per week April 2016 (£)	Spending on UK Minimum Income Standard – net income per week July 2016 (£)
Miscellaneous goods and services (including hair, toiletries, contents and appliance insurance)	18.30	18.30	
Other expenditure items (principally, mortgage interest payments, Council Tax, presents and donations)	50.80	50.80	
Total	427.00	381.00	285.00

These benchmarks for income and spending will be applied, in the chapters that follow, to the people interviewed in Cornwall, for all of whom names and locations have been changed to protect their identities. They are not a statistically valid sample but are typical of those I work with.

Figures on benefits and spending can be dry, impenetrable and a trigger for readers to 'switch off'. These, hopefully, are not and will help build a picture of life for adults with a learning disability. Equally important, however, in the case studies below – all arising from my work as a volunteer advocate - are the experiences of those individuals affected by austerity-driven cutbacks.

The Quiet Man Next Door

Frank lives in a Cornish town on a tight crescent of council housing. On one of my visits to him, clouds are breaking to let the sun filter through. A little like his face as he opens the door he has just unlocked: an initial blankness, a delay in his reactions, gives way to a broad smile, a shrug of the shoulders and a return greeting that is as scrupulously polite as always – 'Lovely to see you too'. Scrupulous and appropriate, unlike the phone call three days earlier when he answered my 'Hello, Frank, it's Neil - Neil from Truro', with 'Hello, Neil from Truro'.

He lets me in and carefully shuts the door behind him, apologising for the fact that he was late in answering and for still finishing off an apple. Immediately, it's my turn to apologise for having stepped off the mat without taking off my shoes and placing them on the newspaper beside his three pairs, two well-polished and one muddy from his gardening.

I wait in the kitchen while he begins to clear up his lunch, the badly burnt remnants of cheese on toast. As they drop into the bin, he tells me he normally likes the taste for 'its added flavour'.

The room reminds me of my parents' kitchen when I was a child: small but with enough space for a compact Formica table and a metal sink with a plastic draining rack, below a latticed window that looks out onto the yard and three carefully aligned recycling boxes.

He offers me a drink. When I opt for a glass of water, he makes himself, as usual, a cup of tea, methodically and turning to answer my questions at the end of each stage: finding his cup, separating the tea bag, putting on the kettle … After five minutes or so, the drink is made.

He resumes his clearing up at a leisurely pace. At my prompting, he tells me about his day at the gardening project and a visit to the supermarket with his Mencap support worker, Martin. His own words trigger a recollection from the previous week – having to go with Martin to the doctor's for treatment on an insect bite that had ballooned up on his leg after his day at the project.

He is, however, far more interested in what I have been doing: whether and where I've seen Gordon Christie (a fellow advocate), the route I've taken to his flat, what I'm growing in the garden, the ages of my grandchildren, what I'm having for my meal that evening (he often asks me if my 'tea will be on the table' when I get home), the personal, the concrete. Some of the questions I've answered on previous visits and an occasional detail in what I say jogs his memory. Whatever the subject, though, each question stalls his wiping of the stacked dishes.

Eventually, the draining board is clear and, at my suggestion, we move into his sitting room. Beside a stack of CDs, the television is on. Local papers and recent mail sit on the coffee table and the arms of the settee. He tells me about a letter he has received – from South West Water, he thinks – but he cannot find it in any of the piles. I reassure him that it will resurface once we have finished our drinks.

Frank is single and in his late forties. He was born near London but in his early twenties moved to Cornwall and away from his parents to be independent and, as he put it, 'for the sea air'. Initially, he lived in a care home for adults with a learning disability but in 2002 moved on his own to a flat where he has lived ever since.[28]

His health is good. He plans his meals well: he eats plenty of salad, avoids food like pasties because 'they've got a lot of salt in them' and a typical Sunday lunch that he prepares is a pork steak with a jacket potato and vegetables. He gets regular exercise, using a bike and sometimes walking three or four miles, each way, to see a friend. A few years ago, however, he had a pacemaker fitted and this has affected his self-confidence, with the line, 'If I'm still here, next year', cropping up in most of the visits I've made to see him.

He has what many would describe as a mild learning disability. Although he has never had a formal diagnosis, he has a number of traits that would often be found in someone who is autistic: love of routine, anxiety and certain conceptual problems. For instance, despite his wide vocabulary – similes such as 'black as the ace of spades' crop up frequently in his conversation and he'll follow and use adjectives like 'innocent' and 'official' with confidence - he can struggle with other words. On one visit, we spent ten or fifteen minutes at his instigation looking at 'autism' and 'autistic' before we established that there wasn't the fundamental difference in meaning between them that he had thought there was. For whatever reason, the idea that the same concept could be conveyed in different forms of the same word had eluded him.

He also finds other, broader concepts difficult to grasp. For example, when I tried to explain the purpose of my book, he found it hard to comprehend the idea of a wide group of people, those with a learning disability across the UK, being treated unfairly. My rephrasing it as people like him getting a bad deal was just greeted with the words 'Deal or no deal' and a big smile.

Another aspect of his disability is very shaky memory: at our first meeting he asked where my wife worked and what jobs my son and daughter have, only to ask the same questions at subsequent meetings. Sometimes, joking prompting will help him recover the answers to such queries but not always.

A further difficulty he has is with timekeeping, despite both his diary that he keeps in strong, clear handwriting and his concern for precision over the timing of arrangements and appointments. He can be late for those same appointments and can lose concentration on what he is doing, a tendency to 'daydream', as he described it.

These difficulties have coloured his employment record. Because of good qualifications in horticulture gained at college, he had paid employment in the early 1990's with Cornwall Council's parks and gardens service as a gardener. Council cutbacks meant that he lost his job, after which he worked as an unpaid volunteer for a firm growing shrubs such as rhododendrons for export and for sale in supermarkets.

He moved from there to work one day a week for three years, again as an unpaid volunteer, at gardens nearby. Of all the places he has worked, this was the one he enjoyed most, mainly for the beauty of the grounds but also for an annual social event at Christmas to which he was invited. He was, however, asked to leave because of poor timekeeping and his 'daydreaming', with the final straw being his pruning a shrub too severely. These reasons may well have been linked: once in a 'daydream', his problems are compounded as he loses track of any queries he might have wanted to raise with a supervisor.

For the last year, he has volunteered, unpaid again, at a gardening project supporting a range of adults, including those with a learning disability. While he enjoys the project, he remains highly critical of himself for losing his previous position at the gardens. He never blames anyone else for what happened but relates, always in a calm near-monotone, how he feels annoyed with himself for his 'stupidity'.

All of these positions he found by himself, with the help of support workers but not of his family who live too far away. He is in touch occasionally with his parents – in a typical year, they come down to visit him once and he goes back up to stay with them, normally also once, often at Christmas. Apart from his brother who works as a solicitor in Manchester and whom he sees 'once in a blue moon', they are his only immediate family.

He keeps in touch with a small range of friends locally, mainly men also with a learning disability. He knows his neighbours only as acquaintances to nod to rather than as friends and sometimes attends a nearby church to which he moved in the hope that he would meet people from a wider age range than at his previous one.

His most frequent personal contact is therefore with Martin who calls in, on average, for three hours a week. While the benefits specified later in this chapter are vital in enabling Frank to maintain his independence, of equal importance is the level of support he receives - with annual assessments being carried out to see how much he needs and how much he should contribute towards the cost of that support (at the moment, like Les in the chapter that follows, he pays nothing). In 2007, the contract for fifteen hours a week which at that point were provided by Mencap was transferred to another organisation, through whom at its lowest point Frank then received a weekly visit of twenty minutes from someone with whom he hadn't built up a relationship of trust. After three years of a campaign involving Frank and others similarly affected, as well as advocates and the local MP, the contract was returned to Mencap but at a level of six hours a week that continued until 2015. Since then, the hours have been halved to their current level.

This drop in support has an obvious personal effect on someone like him – his calm reaction to the most recent cut was 'I feel totally left out' - and its roots are clearly financial: the budgetary pressures Cornwall Council is experiencing because of central government cutbacks. When people have needs and circumstances that are unlikely to change, however, it is hard to justify such an annual assessment process on ethical rather than cost-cutting grounds.[29] When you see the stress that it creates for someone like Frank, it is even harder to justify.

As for his benefits, in April 2016, his total weekly income, on which he didn't pay tax, was £158.70, made up of Disability Living Allowance (DLA) Lowest Care/Lower Mobility at £43.60 and Employment and Support Allowance (ESA) at £115.10. How he spends that income is shown in Table 3 below.

Table 3 - Frank's Spending Compared with Figures Given Earlier in Table 2: Possible Spending, Living on UK and Cornwall Median Income or on the UK Minimum Income Standard

	Spending on UK full-time, median net pay per week April 2016 (£)	Spending on Cornwall full-time, median net pay per week April 2016 (£)	Spending on UK Minimum Income Standard – net income per week July 2016 (£)	Frank's spending per week (£)
Food and non-alcoholic drinks	29.00	29.00		39.21
Alcoholic drinks and tobacco	24.49	18.36		1.75
Clothing and footwear	8.50	8.50		5.50
Housing (net), fuel, power and water	66.30	66.30		33.11[30]
Household goods and services (furniture, appliances, cleaning materials etc.)	19.20	19.20		11.00[31]
Health	3.40	3.40		0.50[32]
Transport	36.20	36.20		13.50[33]
Communication (post, telephone etc.)	10.40	10.40		13.02[34]
Recreation and culture (including TV Licence)	91.48	68.58		7.53[35]
Education	1.10	1.10		0.00
Restaurants and hotels (including canteen meals, takeaways, snacks and holidays/short breaks)	67.83	50.86		8.08[36]
Miscellaneous goods and services (including hair, toiletries, contents and appliance insurance)	18.30	18.30		12.40
Other expenditure items (principally, mortgage interest payments, Council Tax, presents and donations)	50.80	50.80		4.17[37]
Total	427.00	381.00	285.00	149.77[38]

In certain respects, the table is not comparing like for like. The most obvious is 'Housing (net), fuel, power and water' which includes his contribution of £5.63 to the rental cost of his flat, with the remainder covered by housing benefit. This cost to him is much lower than the mortgage payments (shown in 'Other expenditure items') or rental costs (shown in 'Housing (net), fuel, power and water') for someone living on UK or Cornwall Median Pay or on the UK Minimum Income Standard. Frank is also exempt from Council Tax. Equally, he does not pay for prescriptions, dental treatment, eye tests or bus travel.

A more accurate comparison therefore can be made if mortgage interest payments and Council Tax[39] are removed, if rental costs[40] are reduced to what he pays and if expenditure on prescriptions, visits to the optician, dental treatment and bus travel is removed from 'Health' and 'Transport'[41].

Table 4 - Frank's Spending Compared with Figures Given Earlier in Table 2: Possible Spending, Living on UK and Cornwall Median Income or on the UK Minimum Income Standard (but with expenditure on mortgage interest payments, Council Tax, as well as prescriptions, eye/dental treatment and bus travel removed; rental costs have been reduced to what he pays).

	Spending on UK full-time, median net pay per week April 2016 (£)	Spending on Cornwall full-time, median net pay per week April 2016 (£)	Spending on UK Minimum Income Standard – net income per week July 2016 (£)	Frank's spending per week (£)
Food and non-alcoholic drinks	29.00	29.00		39.21
Alcoholic drinks and tobacco	24.49	18.36		1.75
Clothing and footwear	8.50	8.50		5.50
Housing (net), fuel, power and water[42]	35.26	35.26		33.11
Household goods and services (furniture, appliances, cleaning materials etc.)	19.20	19.20		11.00
Health[43]	2.88	2.88		0.50
Transport[44]	35.85	35.85		13.50
Communication (post, telephone etc.)	10.40	10.40		13.02
Recreation and culture (including TV Licence)	91.48	68.58		7.53
Education	1.10	1.10		0.00
Restaurants and hotels (including canteen meals, takeaways, snacks and holidays/short breaks)	67.83	50.86		8.08

	Spending on UK full-time, median net pay per week April 2016 (£)	Spending on Cornwall full-time, median net pay per week April 2016 (£)	Spending on UK Minimum Income Standard – net income per week July 2016 (£)	Frank's spending per week (£)
Miscellaneous goods and services (including hair, toiletries, contents and appliance insurance)	18.30	18.30		12.40
Other expenditure items (principally, mortgage interest payments, Council Tax, presents and donations)[45]	23.19	23.19		4.17
Total	367.48	321.48	246.11[46]	149.77

The table reveals a number of facts about Frank's finances: his expenditure (assuming his full income of £158.70 is spent rather than the figure of £149.77 given above) is only 43.19% of the UK median per week, 49.37% of the equivalent median for Cornwall and 64.49% of the UK Minimum Income Standard. As a result of the shortfall, his spending is concentrated on necessities and he is clearly unable to save – a savings account he had a few years ago was closed because it was unused. He has little money left for a number of areas such as 'Alcoholic drinks and tobacco', 'Recreation and culture' and 'Restaurants and hotels' and therefore does not have 'the opportunities and choices necessary to participate in society', a key element of the UK Minimum Income Standard and a point developed in Chapter 9.

Facts and figures, of course, only reveal a part of the picture. His own view of his life and its quality is at least equally important.

In late 2014 and early 2015, that view was almost entirely positive. Despite how desperately tight his financial circumstances appear from the outside and although he would have liked more money to spend on clothes, he still felt he had enough to buy a piece of cake if he liked the look of it or in his words, 'to go into Wetherspoons for a beer'. He was quietly proud of the independence he had achieved living on his own in his flat – he would, for example, point out decorating he had done - and was unequivocal in his praise of the support he received from Mencap. Seeing a familiar face regularly was in marked contrast to his experience for the three years when the other organisation took over the contract: as well as the drastic cut in support time, he also remembers an occasion when he called into the organisation's office for help. No assistance was given and after ten minutes he was asked to leave.

By spring 2015, some cracks were appearing in his positive perspective. He enjoyed the daylight hours with the mix of contacts and activities he had in place. The evenings, however, without a family of his own, he found increasingly lonely, so much so that by May he was briefly considering a move back into a residential care home because of the regular company it would give him. Within a month or two, though, he was no longer thinking on those lines.

From an advocate's perspective, his reaction in 2015 to his loneliness was perfectly understandable but it may also reflect the way his past has sometimes made him favour dependence over independence. This need for others and their help can be hard to shake off. On one visit he asked for help in getting a social worker without divulging the reason because it was 'confidential' – but a little later in that same visit he said he had no problems that were worrying him.

Overall, nonetheless, he enjoys life on his own. It's always hard to distinguish contentment and happiness but his feelings about himself and his life are somewhere on that part of the spectrum.

He enjoys occasional short trips away organised 'very kindly' (as he puts it) by Mencap. A month after a visit to the Chelsea Flower Show in 2015, he could still recall and describe in detail the flowers - varieties of azalea, polyanthus, ceanothus and wisteria - that he particularly liked. The cost, nonetheless, was considerable. He had to cover not just his own expenses but also those of Martin, his accompanying support worker – his travel, accommodation etc. and the cost of his time. In practice, Martin did not expect him to meet the cost of all food and drink but equally, with a rate of pay that is barely above the national minimum wage, he was in no position to be generous.

One consequence of these high costs was that the trip had to be condensed into two days, with just one overnight stay in London and Martin using a sleeping bag on Frank's floor on the night before they left so that Frank's time-keeping difficulties would not prevent them making a prompt start at 5am.

Holidays apart, however, for most of his life at home in his flat he needs a settled routine. That stability can easily be disturbed by the stress that an unexpected letter or phone call creates. In early 2015, he received a letter requiring payment within thirty days of a bill for dental treatment of over £100 despite the fact that the treatment should have been free. After Martin and his immediate superior at Mencap investigated the matter, it emerged that Frank's HC2 certificate, without which he had to pay for any treatment, had expired.[47] If it were not for Martin's intervention, Frank would have been significantly out of pocket and subjected to even greater stress.

A more striking example of the indispensable help given by Martin came during one of Frank's visits to his parents. He managed the train journey from Cornwall successfully but, partly because of anxiety over his pacemaker, couldn't face the return trip. Martin had to travel up to the Home Counties and accompany him on the train home.

In the long term, it's hard to gauge how much this incident has dented his confidence but it may have been a factor some six months later when he had the chance to meet his parents and his brother at a hotel near Bath. He turned down the opportunity to go because he said he had too many friends in Cornwall that he had arranged to see. It's possible this was the case but it seems unlikely as only half an hour earlier he had told me that as a rule he didn't have enough friends to go out with.

We pull up in the car after collecting Frank's prescription. On the way down, he had adjusted the passenger seat abruptly before double-checking if I was 'allowed' to give him a lift. The directions he gave me were precise and helpful, showing a genuine empathy with my unfamiliarity with the town, until unexpectedly he told me where he needed to get out and opened his door. I only just stopped him getting out on a bend with traffic immediately behind.

Prescription, though, safely in his hand, we come back into his kitchen for another cup of tea. I ask him if he enjoyed the rhubarb I brought from my garden the previous week and he says, with no awkwardness, that he hadn't known what to do with it.

We carry on talking while we cut the slightly flaccid stalks into a saucepan. He asks if he could have another lift later and John O'Groats is the destination when I prompt him, the same humour, a mix of the derivative and the original that he had shown earlier when, in an imitation of one of my feeble jokes, he said that I could see him the following Thursday at 11 o'clock – and, after a theatrical pause, 'in the evening, please'. He had been delighted at my amused reaction.

Once more, however, seriousness and routine take over from humour. He turns away from the draining board to note in his diary the real time and date of my next visit. He again wants to know if and when I'm going to see Gordon.

His diary replaced, he reiterates what to do with the rhubarb, breaking the cooking down into stages. I promise to bring some more next time – 'the same day as the EU Referendum,' I say. He is certain that he'll vote and knows where the polling station is – yet when I ask him which way he'll vote, his face still smiles a little but closes. 'I think that's confidential.'

We sit down again briefly before I go. I ask him if everything's all right. He nods and 'Oh, yes, thanks' comes, despite the delay, as a statement of the obvious. 'But I'd like a wife and children. Do you think I could?'

5

'I'd like to see her put up with this'

Six miles away lives Les, a very different personality, someone who would never withdraw into near-invisibility as Frank does. Our first meeting is at Gordon's house and Les walks straight in, no knock, no ringing of the doorbell.

'I've been looking forward to meeting you, Neil,' his hand outstretched, the grip unusually strong. 'Bloody bus, hour late. Traffic lights.' The reasons for his being late multiply. 'You work with Gordon, don't you? He's a beauty. I like him a lot. Have you seen that film about King John?' His voice is clear: there's no question that I've misheard him. As I replay his words to try and get my bearings, Les continues. 'You didn't see it, either, did you?'

Gordon agrees - and his references to Magna Carta and Robin Hood point me in the right direction – but Les's gaze is on me again. 'Right, Neil, what's this book you're writing then? Will it get you into trouble? With the government, I mean.' On his face is briefly a trace of anxiety. 'But that's their bad luck. Bout bloody time too' – and his smile returns.

Les was born with brain damage – what he calls 'a sickness in the brain' – as a result of his mother contracting German measles while he was in the womb. He is single, 63 years old and has always lived in the same Cornish town.

He has mixed memories from his childhood: although he remembers his grandmother as someone he liked, her words - 'you don't want a girlfriend when you grow up' – are the only ones of hers that he recalls. More disturbing is his account of being beaten up when he was 15 or 16 by his father - 'he was a bastard' - and the police being called to put a stop to it. It had started with a ball breaking a window at the back of where they lived. Nothing Les could say could deflect his father – he remembers him shouting 'You're the bloody culprit', trapping him under the kitchen table and kicking him so hard that his ribs were broken.

This was not an isolated incident. He also remembers his father's anger at his losing his first job putting together broccoli crates. He recalls his father chasing him, before he hitched a lift in a lorry for twenty miles and only just escaped.

After his mother died when only 40, a loss he found hard to cope with, he continued in the same flat with his father and latterly his step-mother. He did, however, find her difficult to live with. He's twice recalled to me her unfairness to his sister - 'She made her wear white socks when she was 16' - and finally left in 2001 when his father died of a heart attack.

Les can still piece together fragments of what happened. 'He hadn't been feeling well for a bit …. he'd put his suit on the back of the door …. he said he was going soon …. he'd gone down the hill about five o'clock to the sea with a friend. They stopped near the cemetery – he said he wasn't feeling well. His mate left him by the car park while he went to wash off his boots where the spring comes up but when he came back, he was on the ground. They didn't have a phone so he waited till a bloke in a van came past so they could ring for an ambulance. He was still alive when it came but didn't last much longer.'

His reaction to his father's death still seems confused. He felt 'a bit upset' when it happened alongside a continued anger at the way he had been treated. Whatever the precise mixture of emotions was that he felt, he very quickly moved out. At first, he lived with an older woman under the Shared Lives scheme[48] and then in accommodation that he found very cramped – 'tiny' was the word he used to describe the bedroom he had for nine years. Since 2013 he has been in a one-bedroomed flat in sheltered housing just off a small but central back street.

He much prefers the flat and with the help of one of his support workers does his own decorating. On one of my visits, he had just finished sanding down the walls in his bathroom, sorting out work that 'bloody cowboys' had done. He was starting to cut cracked tiles and their state may have been a factor in his cutting his thumb badly and needing stitches. The tiles had only cost him a knock-down £2 at a DIY store but overall he guessed that his materials for the bathroom at £120 had used up three months of his savings.

The block of flats has a shared garden and a conservatory that provides a communal living area. Company, though, is limited: he still feels he is living on his own and for him the situation was made worse not long after he moved in when the supervisor employed at that time and with whom he found it very easy to talk was made redundant. She had also arranged a befriender from Devon and Cornwall Housing for Les, an arrangement that subsequently fell through after eighteen months because of cutbacks. 'How would you feel? Eighteen months and you just don't see someone again.'

The loneliness is only occasionally relieved by his family. After his father's death, he has had no direct contact with his step-mother and wouldn't want to – 'she weren't no bloody use to anyone'. He is equally dismissive of his sister who he hasn't seen for over ten years. His brother, however, is very different: he lives in Bristol but is in touch with Les regularly as is his sister-in-law who is seriously ill. Once, Les struggled to explain it and confused me when he asked what it was you eat with onions. The word 'liver' was all he needed – 'she's had a bit of it cut away, poor woman'. For him, she is 'lovely' and when she first fell ill his immediate impulse was to send her flowers. More recently, they invited him to stay for Christmas 2015 but he felt – and his glimpse into someone else's thinking was at first a surprise – that it wouldn't be the same, it would all be 'a bit much' for his sister-in-law and it wouldn't be right to go.

Closer to home, he knows key people in his local bank who always help him through issues and ensure he doesn't have the problem he encountered in a nearby town when bank staff confiscated his debit card because for them he couldn't adequately identify himself.

At a more personal level, he has a friend, a little older than him, whom he bumps into quite often. 'I think he's had a disagreement with the bloke next door but he won't say.' He looks at me knowingly, again implying an empathy with someone else's feelings. As well as a 'lady friend, she's a stunner', for whom he is growing a rubber plant, he knows many of the people who live near him – if you walk near his flat, he is sure to greet someone and have a brief conversation in which his friendliness is reciprocated.

This range of contacts, however, is a long way short of what he would like. He always asks when I am next going to visit and during a period when my wife had injured her back, he asked repeatedly how she was, partly because it was something he could relate to but also probably because it was something – a family, a relationship - he hasn't got. That same yearning for closeness shows in his attempts to trace someone who went to the same special school as him. The attempts have failed which is understandable as it is almost fifty years since they last saw each other.

Perhaps as a reaction to loneliness, his typical morning routine takes him out of the house early. He gets up at 6.45 and then, in the summer, goes out after breakfast. He spends as much time as he can in the fresh air. If the weather or light is poor, he may come back to spend some time in the late afternoon in the conservatory but in good weather I often cannot phone him until after 8 o'clock in the evening. If there is a boot sale on in a nearby village, he may use his bus pass to get there but normally walks the three or four miles back home. Because of the amount of walking like this that he does, a hip operation a few years ago that he needed twelve months to recover from was particularly hard to take.

Unlike Frank, if he's in the library and is asked for his home phone number, he cannot remember it, nor can he read or write, with the result that he needs help with something as seemingly straightforward as the microwave instructions for a ready meal. He also has difficulty with counting. When I told him in September 2015 that his state pension would be paid at 65, he wanted to know which month and year that would be for him - he couldn't independently work out his start date. Time, beyond the immediate, he finds hard to grasp in other ways: once, when I was showing him how to feed his rubber plant, I suggested he feed it again in two weeks' time. Straightaway, he was lost and I had to break the time period down into 'not this week, not next week but the week after'.

This difficulty with numbers can affect him financially as well. His pension is paid monthly – twelve times a year. As I explain later, each Monday he takes out £90 for the week but there will be an occasional month that includes five Mondays and his budgeting is thrown into confusion.

He is, though, well-organised in many ways. When I visit, he is always outside on the pavement waiting for me at the exact time we have arranged so that we can get through the locked outer door; and when I leave he is also always concerned that I close the external door securely behind me. A similar thoroughness shows through in his preparations for Christmas. In his massive DVD collection, all seventeen Christmas titles are kept together and he has a box of cards (along with a decorated tree and a festive jumper) ready in mid-November.

His organisation and sense of time can, however, vary: on one visit, he told me almost at once 'you've only got an hour' because his support worker was coming at 11 o'clock but this obvious awareness of time – he looked at his watch a few times subsequently – contrasted with his confusion when another visitor that he had forgotten (the woman who had carried out his most recent assessment) knocked at his door at 10.30 and our meeting had to be aborted.

In the past, he worked for thirty-six years as a gravedigger, with the last part of his council employment also entailing more general care of the cemetery's grounds and nearby roundabouts. Although he appears ebullient, with a healthy colour in his face, his hip was badly affected by the hardness of the ground he had to dig into with a shovel – hence the operation he needed. Partly as a result of this, he retired early but partly also because of the danger of earth collapsing on him when he was digging a grave on his own. For Les, however, the key factor in his decision was consistent bullying by someone he was working with, against whom, to the best of his knowledge, no action was taken. The man responsible had his leg badly broken in a road accident a year after Les retired and, as far as he was concerned, it was 'a bloody good job'.

With more time in retirement, he has a range of interests that are followed with real enthusiasm. His painting of a local boat hanging in his sitting room is proof of an artistic talent that is largely untaught: in the past, he attended a free drawing class at his local gallery but that has long since fallen victim to cutbacks. The alternatives in early 2016 were two Adult Education courses which may not have been appropriate and at a cost of £125 and £135, with Les not qualifying for a concessionary rate, were anyway far too expensive for his budget. To make them even more unsuitable, they were run in towns between fifteen and twenty miles from where he lives. In May 2016, though, he was put in touch with a tutor who gave him an hour's tuition for £15 which had an immediate impact on his ability to draw portraits.

He also has a huge model motorbike collection below framed pictures of cartoon characters and, in the first months after we met, had an obsessive determination to trace the colourised version of 'Sink the Bismarck' – much of our conversation at our first meeting concerned whether I knew of any second-hand shops, internet sites or car boot sales where it might be found. At many subsequent meetings and In most answerphone messages left - each ending, 'It's only Les' he raised the film, persuading me once to email 20 Century Fox to establish if and where it existed. The film would push its way into any conversation: once, when I told him about a visit we had made to friends near London, his eyes lit up. 'They could find a shop, Neil. You could give them a ring.' When I asked him why he liked the film so much, there was no hesitation. 'It's good. You know, Neil, 2,000 men were killed. So they reckon.'

Equally strong is the way he follows Somerset cricket. Several times when I've seen him, he's been wearing his county shirt with Marcus Trescothick on the back (he has three or four other Somerset shirts from visits he has made to Taunton with his support worker) and once asked me what I thought Trescothick was doing on the afternoon when I called in. He knew everything about the opening batsman from his autobiography which his support worker was reading aloud for him each week. He marvelled at Trescothick's hitting in the past and was intrigued to see if Chris Gayle would outdo it. His eyes light up so proudly at any mention of the County Ground that it's hardly surprising he says he would rather live in Taunton than in Cornwall.

This intensity shows itself in many of the views he holds. Where Frank's opinions – and the words he uses to express them – are always gentle and trusting, Les's are frequently strident and sceptical. On the day after Cilla Black died, he was confident the truth was not being told – 'Right, Neil, right. She's too young. It's the same with all of them. Drugs. The same with all of them.' On politicians he is particularly scathing: he usually called David Cameron 'an arsehole – he's never needed to scrape', the government is 'a load of shit' and his local MP is a 'thief'. He sees the money spent by the government on overseas aid as 'disgusting' When I suggest that perhaps the UK can afford such spending as it's a rich country, he disagrees. For him, the country is 'crap' and his evidence is the varicose vein cream he uses. 'Look at this – we can't even make it ourselves. Has to come from Germany or whatever the place is.'

Unlike Frank, whose conversations are slow and punctuated with many pauses, Les listens respectfully to what someone else is saying but quickly follows with a comment of his own which is often at a tangent from what has just been said. When we were talking again about 'Sink the Bismarck', broken up by his queries about when his pension would change and the timing of my next visit, I mentioned that my own father had served in the Second World War on HMS Exeter. Les asked if he was still alive and, seeing my shake of the head, said he didn't believe in another life or God, before asking me if I believed in Father Christmas. In a matter of seconds, we had gone from his favourite film to his telling me that he thought Santa Claus was probably real.

What was certainly real was Les's financial situation which was unchanged from the previous financial year. His total weekly income in April 2016, on which he didn't pay tax, was £192.21, made up of DLA Lowest Care/Lower Mobility at £43.60 and his council pension of £148.61.

How Les spends that income is shown in Table 5 below, in which, as was the case in Chapter 4 on Frank, mortgage interest payments and Council Tax have been removed. Rent has also been removed and the figures for 'Health' and 'Transport' reduced to what Les pays for.

Table 5 – Les's Spending Compared with Figures Given Earlier in Table 2: Possible Spending, Living on UK and Cornwall Median Income or on the UK Minimum Income Standard (but with expenditure on mortgage interest payments, Council Tax, rent as well as prescriptions, eye/dental treatment and bus travel removed).

	Spending on UK full-time, median net pay per week April 2016 (£)	Spending on Cornwall full-time, median net pay per week April 2016 (£)	Spending on UK Minimum Income Standard – net income per week July 2016 (£)	Les's spending per week (£)
Food and non-alcoholic drinks	29.00	29.00		48.00[49]
Alcoholic drinks and tobacco	24.49	18.36		0.00
Clothing and footwear	8.50	8.50		9.00[50]
Housing (net), fuel, power and water[51]	29.63	29.63		28.50[52]
Household goods and services (furniture, appliances, cleaning materials etc.)	19.20	19.20		7.50[53]
Health	2.88	2.88		0.50[54]
Transport	35.85	35.85		7.40[55]
Communication (post, telephone etc.)	10.40	10.40		7.92[56]

	Spending on UK full-time, median net pay per week April 2016 (£)	Spending on Cornwall full-time, median net pay per week April 2016 (£)	Spending on UK Minimum Income Standard – net income per week July 2016 (£)	Les's spending per week (£)
Recreation and culture (including TV Licence)	91.48	68.58		41.03[57]
Education	1.10	1.10		0.00[58]
Restaurants and hotels (including canteen meals, takeaways, snacks and holidays/short breaks)	67.83	50.86		13.50[59]
Miscellaneous goods and services (including hair, toiletries, contents and appliance insurance)	18.30	18.30		10.19
Other expenditure items (principally, mortgage interest payments, Council Tax, presents and donations)	23.19	23.19		3.80[60]
Total	361.85	315.85	240.48	177.34[61]

The table reveals a number of facts about Les's finances: his spending (assuming his full income of £192.21 is spent rather than the figure of £177.34 given above) is only 53.12% of the UK median per week, 60.85% of the equivalent median for Cornwall and 79.93% of the UK Minimum Income Standard. Despite this shortfall, he still manages to save £9.23 a week (this is set up as a monthly transfer to a savings account). Like anyone else, he feels he needs to save so that he can cover one-off payments like the cost of decorating his bathroom in early autumn 2015.

His financial situation has not always been so relatively stable. In 2010, he found himself with a debt of approximately £600 to clear because his pension had increased with inflation but the housing benefit authorities had not been notified. As a result, the benefit had been overpaid and had to be clawed back. A friend helped him to manage the situation – the debt was cleared over a twelve month period – and set up direct debits for Les to cover regular outgoings like utility bills.

After this experience of debt, he is determined that it won't happen again. With his regular bills covered, his way of managing is take out £90 each week on a Monday. He is, by nature, a spender rather than a saver and this can lead to his running out of money: in one Friday phone call he told me that he was doing nothing until the following Monday when he could take out another £90. A partial explanation for this overspending is the relatively high number of DVDs he buys - a temptation he sometimes finds hard to resist.

His spending on food is relatively high, partly because he uses nearby shops but also because he finds cooking for himself very hard to organise. Although he occasionally cooks himself a beef stew with potatoes, carrots and turnip that he makes last for most of the week, he is dismissive of how tedious cutting up vegetables is and so generally relies on convenience food. For lunch, he often buys fish and chips or a pre-prepared salad from a local shop and in the evening he normally has a ready meal or a can of soup, depending on what he's had for lunch. For a bit of variety, in most weeks he has a Chinese takeaway one weekday evening – 'something with fritters', as he puts it, which costs him about £6 – and, every two or three weeks, Sunday lunch in a nearby pub.

His financial circumstances, however, should improve significantly when he reaches 65. He will continue to receive his council pension and DLA, assuming the transfer to PIP is successful, but in addition should receive his State Pension of £159.55 per week, with the precise amount still to be confirmed. Even if his housing benefit is affected and if he also has to make a contribution towards the cost of his support from Mencap, the additional money will increase significantly his current total income of £192.21. This is obviously welcome but highlights how far government policy on benefits has favoured pensioners at the expense of those of working age, a point developed in my concluding chapter.

Les sees his quality of life as very limited. He sometimes understates the effect his disability has on him – 'It's not very nice when you've got this bloody thing' – but for much of the time it profoundly colours his self-perception. He's used the word 'backward' once or twice to describe himself and feels strongly that he's often not been fairly treated by some of his family or by the country and its politicians. Obvious discrimination or harassment on the streets is now rare, although his £90 drawn out for the week was stolen from him once in 2015 and his anger still flares at being pestered by two men 'taking the mickey' out of him in the 1970s until he 'beat the shit out of' one of them.

A more common trigger for his anger is how little money he has left over each month once his bills have been paid – 'and I've worked all my bloody life. It's not right'. If he had more money, though, he finds it hard to pin down what he would do with it. He would like to have a beer every now and then, at home or in a pub, and a car to give him more freedom but in general 'have a better life' is as close as he gets.

Balancing the negatives is one clear positive: the support he receives from Mencap. Like Frank, his hours have been reduced – in his case from six hours in 2015 to five now in a typical week – despite the fact that his circumstances have not changed. He sees this help as essential – 'I couldn't live like this without them' - and views his two support workers as friends. One of them was at school with him and apart from the three-year period (referred to in Chapter 4) when the work was taken away from Mencap, they have been with him since 2004. They work with him to sort out day-to-day issues and have also helped with painting, laying a carpet and installing a washing machine. Away from his flat, they have taken him out for a meal and on longer trips - to a pre-Christmas market thirty miles away and to see county cricket matches at Taunton.

That chance to get away from his immediate environment may soon have disappeared, again as a consequence of financial pressures which push the Council to look at alternative ways of funding adults with a learning disability. In the past, on a trip such as the ones to see Somerset play cricket, a support worker would use a car provided for the residents at a home run by Mencap in the town. Those residents have now been reclassified as individuals funded through 'supported living'.[62] As a result, their money can no longer be simply pooled to provide a meal for a friend who visits - or to give easy use of the car that Les and two others would previously have shared, each putting in three hours of their support time to create a nine-hour day out, at a relatively low cost per mile.[63]

Mencap, however, remains a positive for him – which is not always the case with other offers of help. For a while, he was part of a group that met in a cafe on Saturday mornings but no longer goes, feeling that the coffee was overpriced and preferring his independence.

This independence is often tinged with bitterness – sometimes at his step-mother for the fact that he's now had several years on his own; sometimes at his sister – 'I'd like to see her put up with this. No-one to visit. Nothing to do in the evenings – only the telly.' Bitterness not just at his loneliness - which worsens in the winter when it is harder to get out - but also at the town where he lives and feels trapped: 'There's nothing here any more. How'd you think I feel when I can't get out of this shit-hole? I had a friend with a lot o' money – would've spent it on a bowling alley and all that. What did the Council do? Laugh in his face. And what's it all look like now?'

Whatever the truth of his recollection, it seems hard to disentangle Les's bitterness and loneliness from a form of claustrophobia. After one meeting with him, I was driving home along the coast on a beautiful day and several times his words - 'I didn't ask to be bloody born like this' - rang in my ears. The contrast between my open life and his enclosed existence could not have been more marked.

6

Why shouldn't he have a holiday?

The greeting from the newsagent is as warm as ever. After handing over the copies of 'What's On TV' and 'Inside Soaps', she waits patiently while Thomas puts them in the section at the back of his rucksack.

'Heard you on Friday. Good show again.'

'Thanks.' He puts the change carefully into his wallet. Concentration over, he smiles. 'See you next week.'

A few yards further along the street, the pattern almost repeats itself in the baker's but there are differences. He asks for two extra bags for his pasty so that no grease marks stain his rucksack. He puts it carefully in the middle compartment and his Bakewell tart in the small front pocket.

With everything zipped up, he starts the long walk home.

Thomas is in his early forties and single. Home for him has always been the same Cornish town. Although he now lives independently, he remains in very close touch with his parents who are in their seventies and who in the background handle most of his finances and any contact with organisations like Cornwall Council.

He has Down's syndrome, a condition that despite his positive outlook and determination has affected much of his life from an early age. As a child he attended his local primary school but at 11 went to board at a special school where he stayed for six years. He enjoyed his time there, particularly liking English and breaks such as one in Wales that involved a range of activities – even though he recalls finding abseiling difficult because of vertigo. One consolation he remembers equally vividly was a kiss from a girl that made him feel better.

At 17 he returned for five years to live at home before moving into residential care, still in the same town. He had there a measure of independence in his own flat within a building where there was twenty-four hour care available on site. He stayed until 2013, when he moved out into supported living in a new flat where he has been ever since.

Just on the outskirts of town, it allows him greater independence. His parents have fully equipped the flat (which has a lounge, bedroom, bathroom and kitchen) with furniture and kitchen appliances. If he wants to go into town, he either takes a fifteen minute walk or catches a bus from a nearby stop – or, if the rain is too heavy, rings his parents for a lift.

As a man, he is open and generous. His emotions are never far from the surface: on our second meeting, he said he liked me and when his parents were leaving us in a café, he kissed his father goodbye on the cheek. At a social level, similar qualities show through. He is unfailingly polite in letting me through a door first – 'because you're a guest' – and insisted on paying for our coffees one day even though it was my turn.

His good humour is rarely ruffled. Playing pitch and putt, he shows endless patience trying to balance his ball on the tee before playing a shot and whenever I show surprise at how far some of his shots have gone, each time his laughter is immediate and uninhibited.

As this suggests, he has a strong sense of humour. He enjoys telling jokes and they can come thick and fast. He once asked me to give him a sport as a cue so that he, off the cuff, could come up with a joke. I gave him 'football' and out came 'Why are footballers cool?' My face was blank. 'Because they have so many fans.' 'Swimming' and the rapid response was 'What do elephants swim in? … Their trunks'. It was impossible to catch him out.

Once he feels confident that he knows someone, his sense of humour extends beyond joke-telling. With me in the car, if I make a mistake driving, he will grin and attribute it all to my age. He will, however, scrutinize my face for reassurance that I haven't taken offence and when on one occasion I jokingly told him that I would let his mum and dad know that he was making comments about how old I was, he looked genuinely alarmed.

Life for him, though, is far from a sequence of joke-telling, with each week having a predictable but nonetheless varied pattern – as he puts it, 'I don't like not being busy'. He has a full day at his local radio station on Monday - and on Friday when he presents his own one hour programme of music. On Tuesday and Thursday from 10am to 3pm, he works at one of the town's supermarkets. Wednesday is his day off and his weekends are full: on Saturday, after a lie-in, he does a variety of activities, mainly surfing in the summer, and on Sunday he goes to chapel and plays Scrabble increasingly well with his parents.

As for the work he does, it's all voluntary – for example, in the past he has inputted data onto a computer for his parents. Paid employment for someone with a learning disability is becoming increasingly rare as my other chapters illustrate and even unpaid work is harder to come by in Cornwall for someone like Thomas. A Council Work Placements Officer was lost in approximately 2012 as a result of the cuts and he got his work at the supermarket largely through his own efforts and those of his parents. Anyone without such family backing is unlikely to find a placement – a point developed in my final chapter.

His work at the supermarket was only supposed to be for twelve months but he's now been there for over three years. To begin with, his job was helping people pack their shopping bags, collecting the security tags off the bottles from the tills and putting the 'left overs' (things they no longer want to buy) back on the shelves. More recently, he has moved to the canteen, preparing and serving meals. Working there leaves him tired, partly because of the heat as his body doesn't adapt well to marked changes in temperature, but he much prefers it to standing, as he puts it, 'like a statue' at the front of the store. For him, it has also become more than somewhere to work ten hours a week and he always gets involved in any promotional events or nights out that the store organises.

His days at the radio station are very different. He spends some of Monday sorting the exact sequence of the tracks he's going to play during his live show. He applies the finishing touches at home, transferring what he has prepared by USB pen on Friday. When his show is over, he inputs chart information onto the station's database and occasionally helps out on a later programme.

As background for his work he keeps on his home computer the detail of every Top 20 chart since January 1990, the date when he was first interested in pop music. His enthusiasm is matched by an exceptional memory which makes the computerised record almost redundant. When he wanted me to test his recall, asking for a No. 1 from 1995 was too easy. 'Oasis' came in less than two seconds and a No. 1 from June 1996 took only a second longer to emerge.[64]

His interests, however, are not just sedentary ones. In the summer, he's been learning to surf for several years through a scheme which aims to help adults with a disability and his confidence has built steadily. 'At first, I really liked using a tandem. It wasn't so scary. You knew someone else was there. But now I normally use a board on my own.'

Obviously, he'd much rather be in the water but sometimes it's too rough. If so, one of the things the group does is analyse on iPads how well each person is surfing. He likes this but finds it frustrating when someone else gets preoccupied with the iPad and won't leave it alone. 'That's not what he's there for, is it?' he says with characteristic seriousness.

Although there are therefore clearly many positives in his life, there are also problems. One which he feels, like Les if not so acutely, is a lack of company. He has a younger married brother, Michael, to whom he is very close but who works in Germany and therefore only sees him infrequently. Locally, he knows plenty of people in the town – he normally says hello to another customer each time he goes into the newsagent's and is greeted by name on the street – but these are only acquaintances. Friends are in short supply, a point he was unaware he was confirming by saying to me the fourth time I met him, 'You could be a friend'.

In the absence of such company, he needs in the background not just his parents but his Mencap support workers who see him for ten hours a week.[65] The core of their help is in menu planning. In a typical week, a list of meals is drawn up on a Tuesday, with some of the shopping done then and the rest normally on a Thursday.

This planning helps to make his meals well-balanced and healthy. On Wednesday, he has an evening meal with his support worker that he helps prepare, with lasagne a real speciality of his. At the supermarket, he is given £3.25 on each day in cash to buy a main meal at lunchtime, with a choice of puddings that he really enjoys and, on those days, he just has soup in the evenings. On Friday, he either has from the freezer a meal prepared by his mum or a take-away from the local fish-and-chip shop: fish, beans and mushy peas but no chips which he doesn't particularly like. On Saturday, after meeting his parents for a coffee, he buys a pasty and a cake – normally a Bakewell tart - in town to eat at lunchtime and on Sunday he has a roast dinner, again with his parents, who plate up a meal for him to eat on the following day.

He's quite happy to vary the pattern with a pub lunch, choosing sandwiches or something like macaroni cheese but avoiding any rich food. This, as well as his making chocolate given at Christmas last until Easter, is a sign of his being health-conscious. On one occasion, from a substantial plate of sandwiches he left a lot of bread and said it was because he was concerned about his weight.

His trying not to eat too much may also be explained by the fact that his stomach can easily be upset, especially if he's worried about something or someone. While most of the people he sees are friendly, he has a neighbour who is physically imposing and through his intrusive presence can make Thomas feel his movements are being watched. As a result, when he arrives home he is quick to open the door without triggering the alarm. On one occasion, however, he was only just able to get into his flat before he soiled himself badly. He got himself into the bath but his mum had to come round to clean him up.

He also sometimes worries over less serious things that most of us perhaps would brush off. On the way home after playing pitch and putt on a very misty, damp morning, he was preoccupied by the grass that had coated his shoes and sprayed up on his trousers, mentioning it seven or eight times during the twenty minute journey. Once he got home and changed, though, he was confident that his support worker would clean his shoes and his mum would wash his trousers.

Money isn't something that troubles him although, like Les, he needs help in managing it. In straightforward transactions like the small amount of shopping he does on his own, he handles money well. For example, one Saturday when I was with him he took £3.90 from his wallet to cover the cost of £3.75 for his magazines and a lottery ticket. Even if he ends up with plenty of change in his pocket after calling into the baker's as well, at this level where he has the coins physically in his hand money makes sense to him.

At a more abstract level, where no actual coins or notes are involved, he doesn't understand what's happening. For instance, because his telephone bill is covered by standing order, he thinks his phone is free. For someone like him, the fact that more transactions are carried out by standing order or direct debit is clearly invaluable in ensuring payments are not missed but it can make money seem unreal and remote.

Another financial problem can occur because of his trusting nature. For most of us, our financial management is interwoven with a complex set of values and a sense of appropriateness that seem simple to us: in most circumstances, we would not give money away to a complete stranger. This, though, is exactly what Thomas did when a man came to his door asking for £20 to cover his electricity bill.

Fortunately, such incidents are rare and his overall financial situation – set out below – is stable. In April 2016, his total weekly income, on which he didn't pay tax, was £244.10, made up of DLA Care Component (Middle) at £55.10, DLA Mobility Component at £21.80 and Income Support at £167.20.

Some of that income is swallowed up by the contribution of £53.86 he has to make towards the cost of his support[66]. A comparison with the financial position of Frank or Danny is illuminating. Because of his condition, Thomas appears to have a much higher level of benefits than either of them; once the contribution towards support is included, however, the difference shrinks. In the case of Thomas, what is given with one hand is taken away by the other. The amount he is left with is £190.24.

Table 6 – Thomas's Spending Compared with Figures Given Earlier in Table 2: Possible Spending, Living on UK and Cornwall Median Income or on the UK Minimum Income Standard (but with expenditure on mortgage interest payments, Council Tax, rent as well as prescriptions and bus travel removed).

	Spending on UK full-time, median net pay per week April 2016 (£)	Spending on Cornwall full-time, median net pay per week April 2016 (£)	Spending on UK Minimum Income Standard – net income per week July 2016 (£)	Thomas's spending per week (£)
Food and non-alcoholic drinks	29.00	29.00		30.50[67]
Alcoholic drinks and tobacco	24.49	18.36		0.00
Clothing and footwear	8.50	8.50		10.00[68]
Housing (net), fuel, power and water[69]	30.63	30.63		22.63[70]
Household goods and services (furniture, appliances, cleaning materials etc.)	19.20	19.20		4.07[71]
Health	2.88	2.88		7.37[72]
Transport	35.85	35.85		0.00[73]
Communication (post, telephone etc.)	10.40	10.40		13.90[74]
Recreation and culture (including TV Licence)	91.48	68.58		17.87[75]
Education	1.10	1.10		0.00
Restaurants and hotels (including canteen meals, takeaways, snacks and holidays/short breaks)	67.83	50.86		61.70[76]
Miscellaneous goods and services (including hair, toiletries, contents and appliance insurance)	18.30	18.30		18.29[77]
Other expenditure items (principally, mortgage interest payments, Council Tax, presents and donations)	23.19	23.19		3.65[78]
Total	362.85	316.85	241.48[79]	189.98[80]

The money at his disposal each week - £190.24[81] - reveals a number of facts about his finances: his spending is only 52.43% of the UK median per week, 60.04% of the equivalent median for Cornwall and 78.78% of the UK Minimum Income Standard.

A different aspect of his financial situation – his right to a holiday - has been the subject of a prolonged dispute with Cornwall Council. As has already been explained in the chapter on Frank, someone like Thomas has to be accompanied by a carer on holiday and this means he has to cover not just his own expenditure but also the carer's food, accommodation, travel, salary, night allowance and incidental expenses. The overall cost for one week in September 2012 with a carer he already knew well, at a holiday camp which specialises in catering for people with disabilities, was therefore £1800.

In the following year, that very expensive option was not available because Cornwall Council and Mencap were unable to provide a carer for the week in question. As a result, his parents accompanied him on holiday.

The case they subsequently put to the Council was that either a carer's costs or their own when they were fulfilling that role should be accepted as Disability Related Expenditure (DRE)[82]. In the financial assessment on 14 October 2014, the initial result was that holiday expenditure was accepted as DRE, only for that decision to be reversed shortly afterwards.

Their appeal was submitted in February 2015 and once it was unsuccessful their case was referred to the Local Government Ombudsman later that year. After many delays – most of them in their opinion caused by the Council failing to meet deadlines - a final ruling from the Ombudsman emerged in January 2017. He ruled that some costs of a carer (but not of the parents) incurred in accompanying Thomas on a holiday qualified as DRE.

The ruling is obviously significant not just for the family but for others in Cornwall as the Council should now change the way in which its financial assessments are conducted. The case should also set a precedent throughout the rest of the country on an issue of principle that takes us back to the point made by the Joseph Rowntree Foundation in arriving at a Minimum Income Standard: ' … a minimum is about more than survival alone.'[83] JRF expand this point with explicit reference to holidays: 'As in every wave of MIS research, groups in 2016 said that families needed to be able to get away from home once a year in the UK as a chance to spend time together and have a break from the pressures of everyday life.'[84] Their point refers to families but applies with equal force to a single man with a learning disability.

The application of the ruling, however, has thrown up further problems as Thomas's parents were told they would receive from the Council a list of suitable carers. When it arrived, it was of limited use as it was in fact a list of caring agencies in the county. In any case, even if they worked their way through the agencies, any person considered for the holiday role would have to get to know Thomas. He, in turn, would have to like the potential carer who would also need to be the right age and have the right energy levels to get involved in activities like swimming, golf, disco, bingo and watching Elvis impersonators. The chance of finding someone seems very slim and therefore the role of accompanying him on a holiday will once more fall on his parents, at nil cost to the Council.

The experience of taking on the Council has confirmed their belief that most decisions are rooted in the need to save money. Before their case was even taken to the Ombudsman, the Council's motivation was apparent to them in September 2013 at a public meeting which they attended with Thomas and only one other man with a learning disability accompanied by his father.[85]

At the meeting, those present were told that the Council needed to make annual savings of £17,000,000 and that their cost-cutting would begin with an average loss of £100 per week for adults with a learning disability. This figure may have been a 'negotiating' position but Thomas's parents assumed that those with a learning disability were at the top of the list because they were the softest target, in many cases unable to speak up for themselves.

Fortunately for Thomas he did have family who would act as advocates for him but it has taken its toll on them. Part of that toll is financial. Their regular, weekly expenditure is on the meals, extra clothing and transport they provide for their son. Almost as regular because of the dispute with the Council (which also cost £210 in legal fees) has been the cost of correspondence[86]. Larger one-off costs arose when Thomas moved into his flat which was unfurnished apart from carpets and kitchen units. They estimate that they spent £5,000 initially to fully furnish it, with a further £3,000 spent in the four years that followed. In their view the expenditure is only right - 'Why shouldn't he have good quality stuff?' – a belief that is in marked contrast to what seems to be the prevailing assumption of many in authority and that led to a man moving into a nearby flat with no cooker and only a cardboard box as the unsteady base for his TV.

The toll at times for a couple in their seventies can also be physical, particularly on holiday when involved all day until bedtime in a range of activities like swimming and a disco. More often the tiredness is mental from the demands made on their time: the constant battle with the Council to get a fair deal for their son; the organisation needed to ensure that he has at least one week's holiday a year and is able to spend time with his brother; and the range of responsibilities they still shoulder such as, among many others, arranging hospital, dental and optician appointments, liaising over work placements and ensuring that his flat runs smoothly by, for example, defrosting his freezer.

Breaking down the 'toll' in this way does not mean that they begrudge the commitment they have made and will continue to make - they would never moan - but to provide the background for their anger at the Council's poor organisation and its hitting adults with a learning disability as the easiest first target.

Thomas is proof of how good the life of someone with a learning disability can be if strong family support is there. Yet despite all that backing and the constant fight for him to be treated fairly, it is worth remembering that his expenditure remains well below the Minimum Income Standard set by the Joseph Rowntree Foundation.

How much worse, however, would it be if there were no family or one which lacked the character and financial resources to do what Thomas's parents have done and will do in future? Families of course don't want to hand over all responsibility for support to councils but his story shows how much the authorities have come to rely on that commitment. If it weren't there, as is the case with

Mark in the chapter that follows, who can be sure that its absence would not be used as an opportunity to further reduce the support provided?

7

Luck, not Planning

Approaching the centre at 5 mph along a potholed track, I wonder if the car, coated in dried cherry blossom, will survive. As I pull up, two men wave me down. 'Want your car washed?' Head turned from the pressure hose directed at another car, Mark grins at me. 'Could do with it.'

Five minutes later, the car is cleaner than it's been in weeks. I ask what they'll take as payment but Mark says they want nothing. 'See you later.'

Mark is different in many ways – including age (he is in his late twenties), character and financial circumstances - from everyone else interviewed for this book. He also, compared to Thomas, has a very different pattern to his week as from Monday to Friday for over ten years he has attended a day centre where, for him, there are opportunities in agriculture, horticulture and engineering. The centre has been a source of stability throughout that period even though what was full funding of his attendance is currently haphazard. Half of the money comes from Disability Cornwall but because no-one makes up the other half, the centre manager is left out of pocket.

Mark was born in Cornwall but at 14 was taken into care twenty miles away from where his parents lived because they were unable to cope with him – again very different from the relationship Thomas has with his parents. The straw that broke the camel's back was a dispute about going to school – he remembers shouting 'Fuck that' and throwing his mother to the floor. He nonetheless stayed in touch with his parents, for example working during school holidays with his father on a farm that he was taken to by a volunteer driver. For a range of jobs like picking cabbages and mending fences, he was, for a teenager, very well-paid at over £6 an hour and once he left school began working there full-time. He did, however, eventually give up the work – the only paid employment he has ever had - because he found regular starts at 6am too difficult and moved instead to work at his current day centre where he has stayed ever since.

At the suggestion of the centre manager, he moved at 18 to another residential care home. From there, he moved again before he was 21 to a village fifteen miles away under the Shared Lives scheme[87], an arrangement that suited him because he had support and there were always people around for company.

That all changed abruptly in April 2013. A meeting was called involving him, the manager at the day centre, his carer, a representative from Shared Lives, his social worker and a person Mark described as his 'Sex Offenders Officer'[88]. It was soon obvious to Mark that the Council's plan was to move him out of his Shared Lives accommodation into independent living. When he realised what they were trying to do, he blew up and, at the centre manager's suggestion, left the room to calm down and 'to have a fag or two'. On returning, he accused everyone there of just trying to save money but the decision had been made: at the end of the meeting he was given four weeks' notice to set himself up for independent living.

He remembers the shock of the decision but also of the pace at which other steps had to be taken. He recalls being asked by his carer if he had money in his account and going out shopping for a television and a second-hand cooker that cost £70. There must have been other purchases and in the opinion of the day centre manager who loaned him £20 a day to tide him over, the Council was just washing its hands of him.

The disruptive sequence of the accommodation which followed justified that opinion for him. Mark was not left to fend completely for himself – although he lost his social worker, he was given excellent help for eight weeks by a housing officer - but the arrangements made could not possibly be described as smooth and in his best interests. The lack of coordination and planning in the current funding of his place at the day centre was only too evident in the arrangements made for his accommodation.

To make his first move, he was given directions on how to use the train and his bike to find a B&B in a town sixty miles away. He stayed there for two weeks, living semi-independently. Each day he would catch a train to the day centre, at a daily cost of £9.80, a huge amount for someone in his circumstances, using his bike at either end but arriving late because he was only able to use his railcard on off-peak trains.

He was then found for six months a one-bedroom flat fifteen miles from the centre – much closer and therefore more convenient. His old bed from his Shared Lives accommodation was brought up for him but the isolation in the new flat drove him to drink more and to increase the number of cigarettes he smoked (a dependency he has since managed by moving on to e-cigarettes).

From there he went to live, for almost six months, with the parents of the girlfriend, Laura, he had just met - before amicably, at Laura's mother's suggestion, moving out to a two-bedroom flat shared with Laura and a long-standing friend of his, Bill. The arrangement broke down, however, when Bill invited some others around when Mark was out of the flat and his phone was stolen. Although the phone was returned after Mark threatened to 'murder' the man he knew was responsible, the damage had been done and Bill went back to living with his mother.

The flat was too expensive for Mark and Laura on their own so she returned to her parents' house and he moved on to another one bedroom flat, where his drinking again increased. Some of it could be early in the morning: he remembered being on a railway station platform with Bill, getting noisy and swearing at anyone - like a woman he described as 'an old granny' - who approached them.

Finally, in February 2015 he returned to live with Laura and her parents. In twenty-two months he had therefore moved six times, hardly the pattern needed by someone for whom stability was particularly important. Before these many changes initiated in April 2013 one incident illustrates clearly how he needed a stable, supportive framework: towards the end of the period when he was living in Shared Lives accommodation, a long-standing relationship of his broke up. He recalls himself at the day centre in floods of tears – feeling he 'had had enough of life' - and incapable of working. He was told to go home 'in case you do something stupid' and his answer – 'That was the plan' – showed how desperate he was. He did, though, agree to go home where all he wanted was to be left on his own on his PlayStation – 'I just didn't want nothing to do with anyone'. He remembers doing little else, apart from emerging to eat, for two and a half weeks.

Within a little over two years, however, he was being moved out into independent existence despite a vulnerability that had already been exposed in his handling of money and relationships. After running up debts of £296 on a contract phone (he has since moved to a pay-as-you-go mobile) and £193 for Council Tax (including £20 added for late payment and only paid after the threat of a court summons), at one point his financial situation spiralled out of control when the money for his attendance at the centre was routed through his personal budget. He used it to spend heavily on clothes and alcohol and by the time the money was instead channelled through Disability Cornwall he was left with a debt of over £2,000 to clear.

As far as relationships were concerned, he takes what women say at face value, not questioning whether a girl saying she was 18 might be a lie – hardly a good idea for someone on the Sex Offenders Register. Adding to his financial difficulties was the fact that he is easily taken advantage of, especially in the past when women realised that he had money he was ready to spend. The worst example of financial exploitation was when one woman was pressing him to provide maintenance money for her baby. A DNA test proved that he was not the father.

Adding to this vulnerability is ADHD for which he had a diagnosis in his teens. Among the signs of the condition is his difficulty in concentrating on what he's doing if someone else talks to him. His temper, a recurrent issue for him, may also be related to ADHD although he's not sure – as far as he's concerned, 'That may just be me' and at points, like his time at secondary school, a result of his mixing with 'the wrong people'.

This volatility disrupted his education. At primary school, he was suspended for a week after hitting another child and breaking two of his teeth; in Year 9 at secondary school he was suspended again, this time for three weeks, after breaking the nose and jaw of someone who repeated an abusive comment to him; and in Year 11 in Art and Design, after he was tripped up with his pot of paint, he punched the person who had stuck out a foot – 'knocked him clean right off his chair' – and was expelled.

The pattern continued at college on an NVQ Level 2 course in Engineering when another student had been taunting him - 'I was out last night boning your missus'. Mark threw a wrench at him, hitting him in the face and breaking his nose. Another suspension followed.

He admits that he's an easy target to 'wind up' and that he still has a temper – in early 2016 at the centre he pinned someone against a wall in 'the biggest flip-out I've had for a bit' - but generally when it flares now he manages it better by going down to a corner of the field on his own for twenty minutes. He then returns, calmer, and apologises to whoever he has spoken to.

Bluntness, however, remains: at our first meeting, when we were talking inside, he looked through the window and rushed out to tell an older man to leave a bench that had just been painted – 'Get up there – it's just been painted'. A few minutes later, the incident repeated itself, with only the words slightly different - 'Get back in your shed!' On another occasion, when I arrived he went out immediately to tell someone else to get out of the workshop because of the inspection pit there and the danger it could pose - or 'I'll break your fingers'. The man ran away, ungainly but as fast as he could.

As his actions above suggest, he feels 'in charge' at the centre when the member of staff who normally supervises his work is not present. He spends plenty of time in the poly-tunnels – one hot day before I arrived he had spent a couple of hours redoing tomato-planting that had been rushed by two other men – and out in the fields where he can work through the whole two or three day process of ploughing fields, using a rotavator and cultivator as well. The area he most enjoys, though, is the workshop where vehicles are repaired. With the Certificate in Machinery Maintenance that he has achieved through the centre (as well as NVQ Levels 1 and 2 in Horticulture to complement his NVQ qualifications from college), he can carry out a range of repairs, among them putting in a new clutch and rebuilding an engine completely in a tractor as well as putting new blades and bearings on a rotavator.

He hopes to get an NVQ Level 3 in Engineering. In 2014 he enrolled on a two year course at college that would have earned him the qualification but had barely started when he was told that he couldn't continue because he was on the Sex Offenders Register. He remembers breaking the glass in the door on his way out because he slammed it shut so hard at the thought of the years he had left on the Register.

This volatility might make it hard for him to hold down the paid job in engineering that is his target. Even though he has improved the way he controls his temper at the centre, it is often just below the surface. As an example, in 2016 he refused to do a job for the centre manager that would only have taken two minutes. He was threatened with a temporary ban from driving on site – an aspect of his work that he really loves - but wouldn't back down. If this happens with someone he respects and has known for years, it doesn't bode well for a new, unfamiliar employer.

The opportunity may, anyway, not arise. Month after month, nothing in engineering gets advertised. The jobs that are available are mainly for delivery drivers and he doesn't have a driving licence. He plans to take his driving test and while he couldn't afford to run a car of his own, he is hoping that he might be able to drive Laura's mother's car if he was added to her insurance. That, however, is not an immediate solution to his lack of paid employment.

As for the way he lives at home, when he was confronted in April 2013 by the prospect of independent living, he could not see any way that he would be able to cook for himself. Getting back from the centre at about 5.45pm and needing a shower seemed insuperable obstacles in the way of preparing a meal but one positive from the upheaval in his life is the fact that he can now cook – a pizza, a pie and what he describes as a 'bean pot' made with baked beans, sausage, bacon, leeks, onions and a jar of curry sauce. This cooking, though, remains a rarity as almost all of his meals are prepared by Laura's parents.

In his spare time he uses his bike a lot and not just to get to the centre. He often cycles on his own and the furthest he's ridden in a single day is about fifty miles. He feels his fitness has benefited from the exercise but there's no routine predictability about his riding. Although cycle paths are fine, he particularly likes the exhilaration of more uneven surfaces – riding on gravel for him is 'mental'.

Home is quieter. He spends a lot of time watching sport in his own room, often while simultaneously playing games like Grand Theft Auto 5 on his PlayStation. He sometimes joins Laura and her mum downstairs watching darts which is also his main interest outside home. The standard he has achieved is very high: one weekend in the summer of 2016, he reached the last four (out of 527 entries) at a British Darts Organisation event in Somerset where he was watched by a crowd of 150-200 in his semi-final match that he only lost 6-5 to a professional player.

Most of his darts, however, is played in his local pub where no expense is involved apart from the cost of his beer. Trips like the one to Somerset are very different: even with help from Laura and her parents, the three days still meant spending £75. Longer distances for him are a non-starter, partly because of the cost but also because he doesn't handle long train or coach travel very well. He finds it difficult to sleep on the journey, especially on a coach where his interest in Eddie Stobart lorries keeps him awake trying to look out for them.

He is not, though, someone who just thinks about himself. He feels a debt of gratitude towards the centre manager and when an accident near the centre and subsequent police action meant he couldn't cross the road, his first step when he finally got in was to apologise to the manager. On another occasion he spent four and a half days on the manager's car, polishing it and cleaning up the chrome as a surprise in readiness for a car rally. Most strikingly, however, he witnessed a man stealing the donations box from a Cornwall Air Ambulance charity shop in the town where he now lives. On his bike, he chased the man for two hundred yards, stopped him and called the police. Later, he was given £25 as a reward.

One day, two months after we'd first met, he surprised me much more. When I asked him if he'd like children, he first explained that he didn't want any with Laura as it would mean that they couldn't both play darts at the same time. He then shrugged his shoulders – 'Got three already, anyway' – and went on to explain that his two daughters and a son now live in Lancashire with their mother, not someone with whom he had a sustained relationship but 'a different one'. The children are the result of several one-night stands that 'went tits up'.

He has no positive memories of the children's mother. The last time he saw her was in 2013 when he went to the woman's house. He found her in bed with another man – in her words, as Mark recalled them, just 'having a bit of fun'. He knocked the man through the bedroom door and through the glass of the outer door. His recollection of the incident is vivid; it is, however, the last time he has been involved in a serious fracas.

He phones occasionally to check the children are all right and doesn't have to provide them any financial support. He has since said little about them but, as far as I can tell, seems relaxed about not seeing them.

How he could provide money for them is hard to see. His own finances have altered a lot since he was moved out into independent living. Up to that point, each week he received ESA and DLA but once he started living with Laura he lost his ESA because she had a job, with the DWP moving him on to Jobseeker's Allowance (JSA). At points, this income has been put in jeopardy by his bluntness: at one meeting at the Job Centre he 'told them to stuff it' – he wasn't going to 'waste' his time there because he could just as easily find any jobs that were available in 'The Cornishman'. At the moment, though, his JSA is intact.

In April 2016, his total weekly income, on which he didn't pay tax, was £94.90, made up of DLA Lowest Care at £21.80 and JSA of £73.10.

Table 7 – Mark's Spending Compared with Figures Given Earlier in Table 2: Possible Spending, Living on UK and Cornwall Median Income or on the UK Minimum Income Standard (but with expenditure on mortgage interest payments, Council Tax, as well as prescriptions, eye/dental treatment and bus travel removed).[89]

	Spending on UK full-time, median net pay per week April 2016 (£)	Spending on Cornwall full-time, median net pay per week April 2016 (£)	Spending on UK Minimum Income Standard – net income per week July 2016 (£)	Mark's spending per week (£)
Food and non-alcoholic drinks				
Alcoholic drinks and tobacco	24.49	18.36		38.66[90]
Clothing and footwear	8.50	8.50		10.00
Housing (net), fuel, power and water				
Household goods and services (furniture, appliances, cleaning materials etc.)				
Health	2.88	2.88		0.00[91]
Transport	35.85	35.85		15.25[92]
Communication (post, telephone etc.)	10.40	10.40		10.00[93]
Recreation and culture (including TV Licence)	91.48	68.58		4.00[94]
Education	1.10	1.10		0.00
Restaurants and hotels (including canteen meals, takeaways, snacks and holidays/short breaks)	67.83	50.86		1.44[95]
Miscellaneous goods and services (including hair, toiletries, contents and appliance insurance)	18.30	18.30		8.40[96]
Other expenditure items (principally, mortgage interest payments, Council Tax, presents and donations)	23.19	23.19		2.31[97]
Total	284.02	238.02	181.23[98]	90.06[99]

The totals speak for themselves. Despite the fact that it is impossible to calculate precise percentages[100], Mark's financial circumstances are clearly a lot worse than the medians in the first two columns and the UK Minimum Income Standard.

Leaving his financial situation to one side – although the amount of money he has is a recurrent theme in his conversation and not easily ignored - his overall view of his life now can vary from day to day. Occasionally, he feels that he would rather be back in his own flat, free and single, partly because at that point, receiving ESA as well as DLA, he had more money in his pocket. Generally, though, he is very happy living with his girlfriend – it's very comfortable, she helps with the cost of train fares and drinks towards the end of the month if his money runs out and where they live is easy visiting distance from his mother (with whom he now has a good relationship) and his younger, physically disabled sister.

Once when I asked him to compare how happy he had been in the last few years, he gave living in Shared Lives accommodation 9/10, living on his own only 3/10 whereas now he described his feelings as 'through the roof – I never thought I'd be so happy – and all because I went to that darts tournament and met Laura'. He is drinking less than he did in the past, partly because he has less money but partly because he is happier living with his girlfriend and her parents as he always has people around him.

It seems like a happy ending and a vindication of what the Council did in moving him out of settled accommodation into independent living. Even if the initial shock and subsequent disruption that it caused him are set aside, it is hard, however, to see the positive outcome for him as the result of careful planning on the Council's part. He has come through because of the support of his centre manager, his new relationship with Laura and the backing of her parents. In other words, not planning but, to a great extent, luck.

Mark's response when I asked him what he thought would happen to him if his relationship with Laura broke up confirmed how fragile his current stability is: 'getting drunk a lot more, getting into trouble, giving this up,' he pointed to his e-cigarette, 'and onto the fags again. Back to my old ways, I suppose.'

8

The Work Capability Assessment

In the massive greenhouse he cuts a small figure, his size further diminished as he stoops to tend the rocket. He slowly straightens his back, unaware that I'm standing thirty yards away, and walks a little awkwardly to a chair where he sits carefully down. He fumbles in both of his coat pockets but with no apparent success – before turning, seeing me and getting once more to his feet.

Danny is 59 years old and has 'acquired brain injury'[101] as a result of a road accident in 1980. He lost control of his motor-bike and was thrown against a wall. The impact broke his jaw, with part of it cutting into his brain. In the first hospital he was taken to, he was on life support and in a coma for over six weeks. Once he had returned to consciousness, he was unable to walk, crawl or sit up and had lost all memory of key elements in his life such as people he knew well and the school he had gone to.

At his second hospital, still in Cornwall, he was treated in a stroke unit because there was nowhere in the county that specialised in the injuries he received. While there, the first stage in his slow improvement was when he was able to come home at weekends. He still couldn't walk and had knee-pads made to help him crawl. His father did almost everything for him and sleeping was far from normal: he had to lie on a mattress on the floor so that he wouldn't fall and injure himself. Perhaps inevitably because of what he'd gone through, he would have frequent violent rages.

On finally being discharged from hospital[102], despite the treatment he had received the accident had transformed him from an active man in his early twenties to someone with the mental capacity of a child of eighteen months.

Emotionally he remained very up-and-down, alternating between laughing and crying, but progress was gradual if very slow. He eventually resumed walking and some of the problems resulting from the accident began to lessen. For instance, in the early years after the accident, he would feel giddy for three or four days in a row. As time went on, however, the vertigo – which could be triggered by looking up to clean a window or by suddenly turning around if someone called out - didn't last so long, presumably because his brain had partially adjusted to the symptoms.

After several years of such progress, his family tried to help him become more independent. He was offered a flat in another town but on his way back from viewing it slumped to the ground in tears, distraught at the thought because it meant leaving home – and the idea went no further.

Two years later, though, a second attempt was successful. He took on his present one bedroom flat, again a few miles from where his parents lived. To allay the extreme nervousness that Danny felt, his father visited every day, was in frequent phone contact with him and, to cement his new independence, bought him a dog so that he had 'someone' to look after. The strategy worked very well as the dog became a key part of his life for thirteen years and his time there has seen him steadily become more independent.

He gets on well with most of his neighbours although one flat in the small block has had a sequence of tenants who make a lot of noise at all hours of the day and night. He once had to move his bed out into the room to minimise the noise coming through from the other side of the wall. He recalls the incident with characteristic understatement learnt, he thinks, from his father: 'If you didn't laugh, you'd cry'.

The problems are not just inside the building; others have in the past come from boys in their early teens. He has had a window broken three times, once clearly accidental when the boys were throwing stones at seagulls and missed. One incident, though, was equally clearly not accidental. Through his letter box he received a small package covered in bubble-wrap which exploded in his hand when he picked it up. The police have been involved at points but the key factor in tackling the problem has been the Council's putting fencing around the building which keeps the boys away.

He does routine jobs like shopping, washing and ironing. His brother and mother, however, live nearby and they have always believed that you should sort out problems as a family and not rely on others, especially the state. As a result Danny for several years has not had a social worker, with his father (and latterly his mother) often assuming that role.

They give him support in specific areas. His brother has set up direct debits for his major outgoings and helps him with more complex financial issues such as dealing with the DWP. His mother checks the use-by dates on his tinned food and does some cleaning, decorating – using a ladder at the age of 80 – and, despite the fact that he has lost his sense of taste, some home cooking such as cottage pie and apple crumble. He prepares the rest of his meals, heavily reliant on the microwave but not always - Sunday lunch could be roast chicken, potatoes and a variety of vegetables, with what's left of the chicken used for sandwiches during the week.

Like Mark, Danny's weekly routine has revolved around a day centre – in his case for 26 years. He works in one polytunnel and four greenhouses, growing rocket and other salad vegetables. He is helped by others at various points but he is the pivotal figure in what is produced there – so pivotal that he had to change his day off to Monday because the centre couldn't handle without him the heavy orders that come in on Friday.

That said, he doesn't work full days because of a build-up of tiredness. His legs ache if he stands continuously for any length of time and as this makes him feel stressed and under pressure, he only stays at the centre until 1.30. The aching eases if he lies down and he normally does this once or twice a week when he gets home if he's been on his feet all morning - but not at the centre, he says with his off-hand humour, because the manager 'wouldn't think much of it'.

It is, though, a sign of his commitment - 'I get paid by the government. I'm thinking all the time: am I doing the right thing?' - that he normally gets in for 9.25, paying £2 each day for his bus ticket despite the fact that he has a bus pass which would get him in for free later. The same commitment shows during the day. If his work is interrupted by a meeting, he will typically try to draw it to a close with the comment 'I'd better crack on'. As the week wears on, however, his energy tapers off, especially on hot summer's days when being in the polytunnel is particularly demanding.

Walking any distance is a strain for him not just because of his aching but also because of his gait[103], groin and chronic lower back pain[104]. These problems inevitably affect him every day: going to the

40

bus stop in the morning would only take someone without his difficulties ten minutes but because he has to rest on the way, the whole walk takes him twice the time. He once told me with a smile, 'I know where all the benches are', and duly and carefully itemised every one of them. On the way back from the centre, after he's taken the bus, depending on how much he's been on his feet, he sometimes gets a taxi rather than walk home.

Partly because of his physical tiredness but mainly because of 'things going round in my head', he sleeps very badly. At best, in between looking at the clock at regular intervals he catnaps - 'At least, I suppose I'm resting.'

And it's rest he tries to get during the day from Saturday until Tuesday - apart from household chores which can vary in the demands they make on his energy. For example, to do his shopping, he doesn't use a bus because the waiting and the sitting make his legs ache and standing to get off can throw his balance if there's a sudden jolt. He therefore normally gets a lift from a neighbour down and back; sometimes he walks down to the supermarket (on a Sunday when he is less likely to be jostled than on busier days in the store) and gets a taxi back at a cost of £5 because he can't manage what he has to carry; on other occasions – such as a three week spell in the late summer of 2016 – he takes a taxi both ways because of palpitations and feeling breathless.

His neighbour is always helpful and he has several friends at the day centre – but not ones with whom he could go out in the evening. Going to a pub Is therefore unusual and on those rare occasions he says he doesn't talk a lot. The pleasure is limited as drinks are expensive on his budget and alcohol – which he never has at home – can affect his balance. For him, unlike Mark, playing darts is also difficult: it entails standing for a long time which he finds tiring and lifting the dart to the right height can make him giddy.

Other recreation is limited. He has had no holidays or short breaks since his father died – he remembers going to Yorkshire and finding such a long journey in the car uncomfortable - and has a meal out only on family occasions. He never goes to the cinema because it means sitting in the same place for far too long. At home, he watches films, particularly Westerns – 'Rio Bravo' is a particular favourite that he has seen twelve times – but not all the way through at one sitting. If the film isn't one that he's familiar with, he then has the problem when he sits down to resume his watching of remembering what's already happened.

Life wasn't always like this. He was born in Buckinghamshire, one of six children, and subsequently moved to Singapore and to various places in England depending on his father's RAF posting. When his father retired in 1976, the family moved to Cornwall. Work too was different. Before the move to Cornwall, he was employed as a messenger on an army base. After the move, he worked on building sites for a while and, finally before the accident, was a hospital porter.

The accident changed everything and turned him into someone who is, to use his own word, 'handicapped' but, years into his recovery, he finally returned to paid work. After one job that lasted only a short time, he had another which involved thawing out fish in blocks of ice under a shower. Despite how cold this was and some 'mickey-taking' that he was subjected to, the job was manageable until the premises moved to a town twenty miles away which meant for him a twelve or thirteen hour day starting at 6am. Because of the state of his health after the accident, he was left exhausted by the combination of travel on public transport and his struggle to handle unexpected demands at work. His brother, in a striking analogy, likened Danny's difficulty in thinking under pressure to his own experience working close to a blast furnace and not being able to think clearly because of the intensity of the heat. The 'heat', for Danny, was in his mind but no less intense. As a result, he wasn't fast enough and lost the job.

That, with the help of a County Council Placement Officer, was the start of his twenty-six years at the day centre. He manages what he has to do partly because he doesn't work a full day but also because the staff in a sheltered environment know him well and understand the difficulties he has. Routine – or 'living in a bubble' as his mum puts it - is at the heart of how well he manages his work there because he cannot handle anything out of the ordinary. His mum, in another striking analogy, said that taking him out of the day centre and putting him into paid employment would be like dropping someone who had lived on a desert island into the middle of London.

The same is true of his life at home – hence the help he gets from his family – and it is very rare for him to go beyond the town where he lives. Before his father died, he would sometimes be taken somewhere else for a change. Now, however, a simple car journey is no longer possible: in its place would be a more complex and expensive arrangement with a taxi. The alternative is using the train but he recalls catching one to Truro several years ago and, when it was time to come home, finding that he had walked up the wrong hill for the station. The result was a further mile or so for him to walk, with an inevitable strain placed on his legs and his breathing - and a missed train, with all the stress that created for him.

Even within his 'bubble', he can easily forget things. At home, despite a box clearly marked with the days of the week, he can miss taking his key thyroid tablet – once for three days in a row. His shopping can also fall victim to poor memory. He has found himself ready to pay at the supermarket, only to realise that his wallet is at home. He resolves the situation either by putting all the items back one by one and doing the shopping on another day or by leaving the trolley at the desk and getting a taxi home and back again so that he can pay. Similar problems can affect him at the day centre if a member of staff gives him a piece of paper with a three-item order to be prepared. If Danny puts it in his pocket, he probably won't remember that it's there – so a part of his routine is to put it in the same prominent position on the table in the area where he works. With this, of course, there is always the risk that someone else, thinking that it's a piece of scrap paper, will throw it in the bin and the stress that Danny had hoped to avoid will have been greatly increased.

Stress is a growing issue for him. While he was alive, his father dealt with any such 'mental' issues – an aspect of the family's belief in self-help – with a doctor seen only for physical problems but now what the doctor described as a 'low mood' is under investigation. The stress has been worsened by a range of additional health problems that have developed as he's grown older. Hay fever is particularly unpleasant for him because of his work at the day centre. He has palpitations - sometimes at night but mainly when he feels under pressure - and they normally last for between one and three hours at a time. He's unsure what triggers them. Once (an incident he told me about on three separate occasions, another example of his forgetfulness) he was in the supermarket trying to decide whether to buy lamb chops or lamb leg steaks but couldn't figure out whether the palpitations and the tightening of his chest on this occasion were caused by the pressure of the decision over the meat or by the fact that he had had to walk down to the supermarket, rather than get his usual lift. Whatever the trigger, he takes medication as and when the palpitations occur.

As if these problems were not enough, he has an underactive thyroid for which he is on medication and in 2014 was diagnosed with emphysema which leaves him short of breath. The fact that he has smoked in the past may have been a cause and certainly wouldn't have helped his breathing. On the positive side, however, in October 2016 he was three months into his attempt (his third one) to kick the habit and was hopeful that he was winning the battle; on the negative side, his emphysema was steadily worsening.

Medically, therefore, his condition is very serious, which makes the actions of the authorities harder to comprehend. The first such action removed Social Services funding for his place at the day centre. At a meeting in 2014 which he attended with his mother but not with the centre manager, he was told that in using the placement for 'social reasons' he no longer met their criteria. Danny felt unable to argue his case. Matching 'criteria' and his personal circumstances was too complex for him to reason and talk his way through - in his words, although he thought the decision meant the councillors could 'have a decent pay rise', he couldn't 'see the whole picture'.[105]

Worse was to come from the authorities – and not this time the Council but the DWP. He had to attend a Work Capability Assessment in early July 2016 – the first such assessment he had had since his accident.[106] He remembered the bus journey there with his mother and how afterwards his legs were aching, as a result of which his mind went blank when he went in to see the doctor carrying out the assessment.

His initial reaction – before the result of the assessment came through – appeared to be unruffled stoicism. In a very level voice he mentioned a test that he was given where he was asked to remember three things that were pointed out to him: a ball, a pen - and a couch that was directly behind the doctor in his line of vision. He remembered them – and his ironic recollection of this success was typically restrained: 'That made me mastermind'.

He recalled not handling the pressure created by the questions 'coming off the computer'. When asked about the last time he had had palpitations, he couldn't answer. He also didn't think to give essential facts that would have built a full and accurate picture of his health and the difficulties he regularly experienced – and so when he was asked about his breathlessness, he forgot to mention his emphysema. Afterwards, he said repeatedly that in his answers he couldn't see 'the whole picture'; it was only when he spoke to his mother and brother that he realised all the other things he should have said.

The incompleteness of what he conveyed was worsened by his mother not being allowed to say anything to supplement or clarify each of his answers immediately after he had given them[107]. She had the opportunity at the end of the assessment but only when all of his responses had been recorded. Nothing she said altered what was already written down.

He believed at the time that if the assessment went against him his benefits would still be paid while his appeal was being dealt with.[108] If, at the end of the whole process, they made him go back to work because he'd got 'a pass with flying colours', he would in his own seemingly stoical words be 'dead in a year – it doesn't matter'.

When the result of the assessment did come through in early September, he couldn't maintain his façade of apparent unconcern. He broke down in tears at the decision that he had only been awarded six points in the assessment, with fifteen needed to retain his ESA.[109] Once he had stopped crying, his reaction was scathing – 'you only got to look half-human and you're buggered'. When he heard that he would also be moved on to JSA, his reaction was that he would 'rather be dead' than go through what it entailed[110] because of the pressure it would put on him. 'Who appointed them? God? Worst thing they've ever had is a broken finger-nail.'

As for the detail of the assessment, at various points it failed to show accurately what he could and couldn't do. As a check on his balance, he was asked to do one squat and from there to look up to see if he experienced any dizziness. On that one brief check he 'passed' when doing it for any longer would have shown his problems in both areas. His ability to walk was misrepresented in the subsequent letter: his twenty minute walk to the bus stop resting on benches along the way became, 'He walks at a normal pace to the bus stop - it takes twenty minutes without stopping.' The broader conclusion that Danny 'can move more than 200 metres on flat ground' also overlooked real-world variations in the surface of any pavement that he is walking on. A rough surface can cause him to trip and a slippery or icy surface poses problems for his balance. Any slope in the pavement is another variable that was ignored. Walking uphill puts an extra strain on his breathing; walking downhill is difficult for him because of his balance – a point that also applies to his use of steps and stairs where he is particularly nervous if there is no hand-rail.

The letter also asserted that he 'can usually stay in one place (either standing or sitting) for more than an hour without having to move away'. This was based on the doctor's opinion that Danny 'was able to sit on a chair with a back for seventy minutes, at the assessment' – an opinion which overlooked the fact that he was twice asked to stand and walk to the examination couch by the doctor. This automatically relieved the pain in his pelvic region in the same way that he does as a matter of course by breaking up periods of sitting with standing and vice versa.

The letter and its accompanying medical report misrepresented other aspects of his life. The report stated that he 'denies self-harm' despite the fact that when he was asked by the doctor if he had thought of suicide, he said he had but that he didn't know how to do it. The conclusion that he could 'convey a simple message to strangers' overlooked his difficulty in finding words which in his own doctor's opinion has sometimes resulted in his getting involved in a dispute. Danny confirmed that opinion: if someone asks him two questions in rapid succession before he has sorted out the first in his mind and found the words he needs, he just tells the person concerned to 'piss off'.

The list could go on but perhaps the key point was made by Danny's brother at the end of his letter asking for a reconsideration of the decision: 'When I see no fundamental change in Danny, I am at a loss to understand why ESA should suddenly be taken away from him, especially as he is now approaching the age at which the neurologist treating him after his accident in 1980 said that his condition would begin to worsen.' For Danny it was simpler. After the accident, he had managed to 'build up' a life; 'now they're just taking it away'.

The 'Mandatory Reconsideration'[111] process was demanding for the whole family: putting together arguments against the decision; getting supporting statements from the day centre, Danny's chiropractor and his doctor (whose written comments cost £17.50); and finally drafting the letter so that it was sent in before the deadline. Hard work and additional expense were, of course, only two elements in the preparation. Far more significant was the strain created for the family – and particularly for Danny.

The case made for reconsideration was successful – and, fortunately, almost immediately. His family's letter was dated 4 October 2016 and the reply restoring his ESA was sent three days later. A naïve reaction would be that the speed of response indicated a recognition of the obvious error made in the initial assessment. A more cynical reaction to the speed would be that the DWP had prepared itself to overturn the initial judgment on Danny's case, a cynicism backed up by the high success rate of appeals: according to the government's own statistics, approximately 59% have been successful[112] and this is after a number of assessments have already been reversed at the 'Mandatory Reconsideration' stage. Such evidence suggests that the system is fundamentally unfair to those on benefits, with 'successes' of people like Danny and the administrative costs incurred along the way accepted by the DWP if it means that a significant number of other people are removed from ESA and the government makes an equally significant financial saving.[113]

In mid-October 2016, therefore, Danny's total weekly income, on which he didn't pay tax, was once more what it had been six months earlier - £160.10, made up of DLA Lowest Care/Lower Mobility at £43.60 and ESA at £116.50[114].

Table 8 – Danny's Spending Compared with Figures Given Earlier in Table 2: Possible Spending, Living on UK and Cornwall Median Income or on the UK Minimum Income Standard (but with expenditure on mortgage interest payments, prescriptions and bus travel removed; rental costs and Council Tax have been reduced to what he pays).

	Spending on UK full-time, median net pay per week April 2016 (£)	Spending on Cornwall full-time, median net pay per week April 2016 (£)	Spending on UK Minimum Income Standard – net income per week July 2016 (£)	Danny's spending per week (£)
Food and non-alcoholic drinks	29.00	29.00		37.66
Alcoholic drinks and tobacco	24.49	18.36		0.50[115]
Clothing and footwear	8.50	8.50		7.21
Housing (net), fuel, power and water[116]	36.96	36.96		22.99[117]
Household goods and services (furniture, appliances, cleaning materials etc.)	19.20	19.20		8.80[118]
Health[119]	3.31	3.31		11.07[120]
Transport	35.85	35.85		16.00[121]
Communication (post, telephone etc.)	10.40	10.40		7.13[122]
Recreation and culture (including TV Licence)	91.48	68.58		14.32[123]

	Spending on UK full-time, median net pay per week April 2016 (£)	Spending on Cornwall full-time, median net pay per week April 2016 (£)	Spending on UK Minimum Income Standard – net income per week July 2016 (£)	Danny's spending per week (£)
Education	1.10	1.10		0.00
Restaurants and hotels (including canteen meals, takeaways, snacks and holidays/short breaks)	67.83	50.86		1.20[124]
Miscellaneous goods and services (including hair, toiletries, contents and appliance insurance)	18.30	18.30		10.58
Other expenditure items (principally, mortgage interest payments, Council Tax, presents and donations)[125]	30.66	30.66		10.16[126]
Total	377.08	331.08	255.28[127]	147.62[128]

The table reveals a number of facts about Danny's finances: his spending (assuming his full income of £160.10 is spent rather than the figure of £147.62 given above) is only 42.46% of the UK median per week, 48.36% of the equivalent median for Cornwall and 62.72% of the UK Minimum Income Standard.

His feelings about his financial situation fluctuate. Sometimes his stoicism resurfaces when asked about the small amount he has left over at the end of the week: 'Oh, I'm all right'. At other times a different voice emerges. He once sized it all up without a trace of self-pity when he said he'd rather die: 'This i'nt life – it's no fun.'

Alongside his feelings, critically important as they are, an outsider's perspective needs to be added. The other case studies in this book reveal the wide range of problems that austerity has created for adults with a learning disability. Danny's story, however, has been saved to the end because of the extreme nature of the insensitive and illogical way in which he has been treated – another result of austerity.

9

Wellbeing: the Reality

When I began work as a volunteer, one of my strongest initial impressions as I went to different day centres or visited people at home was how poor almost everyone seemed, as if poverty was an inevitable part of having a learning disability.

My initial impression is consistent with one of the conclusions reached by the Joseph Rowntree Foundation in its report 'Monitoring Poverty and Social Exclusion 2016': 'Once account is taken of the higher costs faced by those who are disabled, half of people living in poverty are either themselves disabled or are living with a disabled person in their household.' The impression was further confirmed by one of the findings in the press release accompanying the publication of 'Being Disabled in Britain: A Journey Less Equal' by the Equality and Human Rights Commission: 'Families in the UK with a disabled member are more likely to live in relative poverty than non-disabled families.'

Relative poverty according to the most widely used definition is when a household's income is below 60% of UK median household income. While the data I have used concerns spending rather than income, the one is clearly derived from the other – and the spending of all four men[129] shown in Table 9 is below 60% of the UK median, the relative poverty threshold.

Table 9 – Spending of Those in the Case Studies as a % of the Spending of Someone Living on UK and Cornwall Median Income or on the UK Minimum Income Standard

	Spending on UK full-time, median net pay per week April 2016 (%)	Spending on Cornwall full-time, median net pay per week April 2016 (%)	Spending on UK Minimum Income Standard – net income per week July 2016 (%)
Frank	43.19	49.37	64.49
Les	53.12	60.85	79.93
Thomas	52.43	60.04	78.78
Danny	42.46	48.36	62.72
Average	47.80	54.66	71.48

For each of them, such limited spending power has a direct impact on his life, the quality of which should be much more than mere survival, a point made by not only the Joseph Rowntree Foundation but also the 2014 Care Act. In the definition of the Minimum Income Standard, social needs – such as company and 'the opportunities and choices necessary to participate in society'[130] – have to be met as well as the basics (such as food and a roof over your head) required to sustain independence. The same concept, in slightly different wording, is reinforced in the 2014 Care Act, with its emphasis on wellbeing: 'Local authorities must promote wellbeing when carrying out any of their care and support functions in respect of a person. This may sometimes be referred to as the wellbeing principle because it is a guiding principle that puts wellbeing at the heart of care and support.'[131]

The Act identifies key components of wellbeing, many of which go beyond what is necessary for bare survival. 'Wellbeing is a broad concept, and it is described as relating to the following areas in particular: personal dignity (including treatment of the individual with respect); physical and mental health and emotional wellbeing; protection from abuse and neglect; control by the individual over day-to-day life (including over care and support provided and the way it is provided); participation in work, education, training or recreation; social and economic wellbeing; domestic, family and personal; suitability of living accommodation; the individual's contribution to society.'[132]

The authorities are falling short of 'promoting' wellbeing in many of these areas for the men in my case studies. Their 'participation in work' is limited, with an obvious effect on their ability to live independently – and as the Care Act puts it, 'the concept of independent living is a core part of the wellbeing principle'.[133]

'Recreation' and 'social and economic wellbeing' are other areas in the Care Act's description of the principle where their opportunities are limited. Two categories in Tables 3-8 - 'Recreation and culture' and 'Restaurants and hotels', an ironically grandiose term to describe where their money goes - are particularly important in establishing their ability to have 'the opportunities and choices necessary to participate in society' (the Minimum Income Standard definition)[134].

Table 10 - Spending of Those in the Case Studies on 'Recreation and Culture' as a % of the Spending of Someone Living on UK and Cornwall Median Income[135]

	Spending on UK full-time, median net pay per week April 2016 (%)	Spending on Cornwall full-time, median net pay per week April 2016 (%)
Frank	8.23	10.98
Les	44.85	59.83
Thomas	19.53	26.06
Danny	15.65	20.88
Average	22.07	29.44

Table 11 - Spending of Those in the Case Studies on 'Restaurants and Hotels' as a % of the Spending of Someone Living on UK and Cornwall Median Income

	Spending on UK full-time, median net pay per week April 2016 (%)	Spending on Cornwall full-time, median net pay per week April 2016 (%)
Frank	11.91	15.87
Les	19.90	26.54
Thomas	90.96	121.31
Danny	1.77	23.60
Average	31.14	46.83

Tables 10 and 11 show how limited the ability of the four men is to 'participate in society'. Even though the average in Table 11 is greatly inflated by the amount Thomas sets aside for a holiday, their expenditure is still well below national and county norms.

Financial data, however, only gives a partial picture. Under 'Recreation and Culture', Les has the highest spending, close to the Cornwall median, but all his money goes on solitary interests. While Thomas uses most (but not all) of his money in this category in the same way, Danny and Frank (whose £7.53 a week in this area in Table 4 is strikingly low) are like Les, spending nothing with other people.

A similar pattern emerges in the detail behind the raw figures on 'Restaurants and Hotels'. While Thomas has meals with others at the supermarket and Danny's very small amount is used up only on meals out with his family, Frank and Les eat virtually every meal out on their own. The same applies to the occasional beer that Frank has in Wetherspoons: he almost always drinks alone.

In both categories, they are clearly not in most instances 'participating' (in the full sense of this key word for both the Minimum Income Standard and 2014 Care Act) in society. Put simply, they lack company (a key word again for the Minimum Income Standard) and as a result loneliness becomes an issue. Friends are thin on the ground for Thomas and Danny; despite the independence he has achieved and the resultant ability to make decisions for himself, Frank has contemplated moving back into residential care because of his loneliness in the evenings; and Les rails constantly against having to live on his own.

'Participation', therefore, like employment, 'recreation' and 'social and economic wellbeing' is an area in the Care Act's description of wellbeing where the men fall short of what most of us would expect. To an already long list can be added the way they all lack control 'over day-to-day life': each has experienced a cut in the number of hours he receives as support or in the funding for his placement at a day centre.

Perhaps most tellingly, as an indicator of the gap between the language of the Care Act and the reality of government policy, for 'personal dignity' could anyone be shown less 'respect' than Danny in his Work Capability Assessment or less concern for his 'mental health and emotional wellbeing'? The gap is huge.

10

Austerity: the Villain of the Piece

The obvious questions arise for adults with a learning disability. In spending power, why are they left so far behind in this country?[136] Why is their support declining? Why is there such a gap between rhetoric and reality?

Among the answers is their profile in our communities. Not only are they 'buried' in statistics, they are relatively invisible compared to older people and wheelchair users. We can all recognise a wheelchair; most of us have a relative who is over 60; but almost no-one would see someone like Danny in the street and think he had a learning disability. This profile is not helped by the media: coverage of Adult Social Care underfunding on television and in the press has a focus on provision for the over-sixties rather than those with a learning disability and so their needs are hidden even further from view.

The other answers don't lie just in policies implemented since 2010. Some trends originated long before the coalition. Outsourcing of specific areas of activity to an 'arm's length' company has been a feature of the national and local government landscape for many years. This does not merely create confusion over just who is responsible for what across a wide spectrum of services but has a direct bearing on provision for adults with a learning disability in Cornwall.

For example, at the moment, CORMAC is a company still wholly owned by Cornwall Council but whose core area of work is responsibility for the upkeep of the county's roads. It has, however, itself now developed a small scale domiciliary care service – CORCARE – that provides services in their own homes for Cornish residents including those with a learning disability, an area that would once have been the direct responsibility of the Council itself.

In such companies – and CORMAC is only one example - because of the pressure of cost-driven competitive tendering and because the learning disabled are not at the heart of their activities, there is clearly a risk, no matter how high the quality of staff on the ground, that the 'clients' can be seen as peripheral to the need to make a profit. In 2007, this must have been the case when responsibility for Frank's weekly support was transferred from Mencap to a new organisation and as a result he went from receiving fifteen hours a week from people he trusted to twenty minutes, at its worst, from someone he had never met before.[137]

Most of the answers, however, to the problems encountered by adults with a learning disability can be found in the governments' austerity policies since 2010 which have created a financial squeeze on local authorities[138] and consequently on the organisations that provide services for them. Andrew Cannon, CEO of Voyage Care[139] and co-chair of Learning Disability Voices[140], explained in an article in the Guardian on 25 May 2016 how severe that impact had been: 'For five years, we have had to cut fees for local authorities, which have had to make spending cuts of about 40%. Now some smaller organisations are closing services they can no longer afford to deliver. Larger providers are being asked to step in to take over affected individuals' care packages. But for how long will they be able to do this?'[141]

His opinion was confirmed in the publication in early July 2016 of a survey conducted by the Association of Directors of Adult Social Services (ADASS). It revealed that government cuts had resulted in a £4.6bn reduction in social care budgets in England since 2011. In the words of Harold Bodmer, president of ADASS at the time, 'Services are already being cut, and the outlook for future care is bleak. We're at a tipping point where social care is in jeopardy, and unless the government addresses the chronic underfunding of the sector, there will be worrying consequences for the NHS and, most importantly, older and disabled people, their families and carers.'[142]

Early in 2017, the Local Government Association related the underfunding to its duties under the Care Act and in particular to the concept of wellbeing – and the gap between that concept and the financial reality - already highlighted in Chapter 9. 'In its submission to the Treasury ahead of the Spring Budget, the Local Government Association, which represents more than 370 councils in England and Wales, says the continued underfunding of social care is making it impossible for local authorities to fulfil their legal duties under the Care Act, leaving it on the brink of failing altogether and councils facing the prospect of court challenges.

'The LGA says the funding crisis in social care is threatening the very spirit of the legislation which is about supporting people's wellbeing and helping them to stay well and live dignified, independent lives.'[143]

Cannon, Bodmer and the LGA were not scare-mongering. The impact of this funding crisis in Devon and Cornwall was twice highlighted on Spotlight (the BBC's local television news programme for the south-west) in March and April 2017. On 21 March, its focus was on Trelawney Domiciliary Care, an organisation based in Camborne that provides care for a range of men and women including those with a learning disability and that now cannot make a profit from the services it provides.

On 4 April, its lead story was that two Hft homes in Devon were to shut at the end of the month, with one man who had lived there for twenty-seven years having to move out. The programme saw Hft's situation as symptomatic of the problems other providers were experiencing, with a figure quoted of 55% of learning disability providers expecting to run at a loss within two years. Robert Longley-Cook, Chief Executive of Hft, attributed these financial difficulties to two key factors: first, the pressure councils were under which meant that their funding for services provided by people like Hft was cut; and second, costs which by 2020 were expected to rise by 50%, principally because of the National Living Wage, pension auto-enrolment and the apprenticeship levy.

Against such a financial background, it is not surprising that the percentage of people receiving long term support from local authorities across the country appears to be declining. For example, Table 12 below shows that while the number of adults with a learning disability in Cornwall known to the local authority is increasing, the number receiving long term support is relatively constant.[144]

Table 12 - Long Term Support for Adults with a Learning Disability

	Total number of adults (18 to 64) with a learning disability in Cornwall known to the local authority	Total number of adults (18 to 64) with a learning disability getting long term support from Cornwall Council	% of adults (18 to 64) with a learning disability getting long term support from Cornwall Council
2014-15	2224	1607	72.26
2015-16	2411	1672	69.35
2016-17	2484	1629	65.58

Even for those who are still receiving support, the picture is hardly rosy. Being recorded as 'getting long term support' doesn't mean that it remains the same – as the cuts for Frank, Les and Thomas demonstrate. The basis on which it is given can anyway be fundamentally illogical: a disabled man can receive none because he is deemed capable of living without it; he receives a Capability for Work Questionnaire which he fails to complete, largely because he doesn't have a support worker in place to help him; non-completion means that his benefits are reduced or removed; and as a final consequence he finds himself in a situation where support is essential for him to find a way out of the dire financial circumstances that are now his lot.

How much less traumatic to provide sustained help at the appropriate level in the first place, particularly as the financial consequences of inadequate support can be exacerbated by exploitation? Bad as the debts of Les and Mark were – approximately £600 and £2,000 respectively – they pale alongside the difficulties experienced by Sally, a woman living near Mark and at that point without any support. She was sold four credit cards, three of them Barclaycards. Having been told she only needed to make the minimum payment each month and with no understanding of compound interest rates, she subsequently ran up debts of over £20,000.

It was only when Cornwall Council Adult Social Care called in Mencap that the extent of her debt was discovered. After using a debt recovery firm, her new support workers threatened to contact the Financial Services Ombudsman over the conduct of the banks whose original offers would have taken her twelve years to clear. The pressure applied to the banks worked, the debts were written off but the trauma has left her reluctant to answer the door or the phone for fear of being exploited again.

As this reaction of hers shows, the consequences of inadequate support are not just financial but psychological. Such insecurity is evident throughout my case studies: the preoccupation of Frank and Les with locking their doors is one manifestation of this; the exit sensor and panic button that Thomas has are further signs; and Danny having to deal with an exploding package posted through his letterbox is an extreme example of the real problems that can create this insecurity. In such circumstances, there is none of the relaxation that comes from an open door on a sunny day.

If support hours continue to be steadily reduced, someone like Frank or Les could find himself totally isolated and as vulnerable as Sally was because he lacks the kind of close family backing that Thomas receives. For the state to assume that everyone has such backing is to ignore the reality of people's lives. It is also financially short-sighted as it leads to greater expense in the long run, when interventions are needed at crisis points like the one which affected Sally or when stress triggers physical and psychological problems that the Health Service has to deal with. More importantly, however, the failure to fund an adequate level of support is fundamentally unfair.

Decision-making on support is only one area in which mistakes are made by the Council (and almost certainly by other councils across the country). In Thomas's case, an unjust ruling on his right to a holiday is made; in Mark's case, he is given four weeks to set himself up to live independently. For both there would have been other factors involved in the decisions made by the Council but the need to save money because of the financial squeeze from central government was probably the key one.

As a result of the pressure, councils behave in ways that could well have been different in better financial times. The same applies to others working in the sector. One instance concerned Frank who was visited by two people working for other organisations than his current support providers, Mencap, in late 2015. Martin, his support worker, who was with him at the time, assumed that their appointment was offering something over and above Mencap provision and therefore complied with their request that he leave the flat.

In the course of the visit, Frank was given written information on an alternative to Mencap with a focus on general work preparation such as putting together a CV that would have entailed employing a PA to organise the arrangements. Taking up this option as a way of spending the money that he had from the Supporting People budget would have left him with insufficient money to continue with Mencap. The provision offered may well have been of a very high quality but because of its focus would have left him without the regular support he needs.

At the meeting, he was asked to sign a document. Very wisely he didn't as, in his words, 'it was going in the wrong direction' but an arrangement was made for him to go to a later meeting (subsequently cancelled after he had spoken to his parents and the Mencap coordinator) and for him to receive a pack of background information, with a range of forms that required completion so that he would be able to act as an employer and to set up his own payroll etc.

If I, as someone who is used to form-filling, had received the forms myself, they would have made me think twice about the arrangement because of their complexity[145]. The form-filling and subsequent bureaucracy, if the arrangement had gone ahead, would probably have been handled by Disability Cornwall for a fee of approximately £6 per month but for Frank the amount of paperwork was ludicrously high, especially when the end 'product' was not even meeting his needs in the most appropriate way. The absurdity was best summed up in his own reaction - 'Gordon Bennett!'

Such behaviour, however, is not just an absurdity, a laughing matter. It is perilously close to intimidation. Although he was able to withstand the pressure to sign a document, he is nonetheless someone to whom such pressure, heightened by the removal of his trusted support worker, should not be applied. Once more, the concept of wellbeing has been totally overlooked because the drive to compete rather than cooperate means that the needs of adults like Frank are no longer central.

Most of these problems arise indirectly from central government because of its underfunding of council social care budgets; the key area, however, where the austerity imposed by central government has a direct impact on adults with a learning disability is its policy on benefits, which has produced a relative decline in working age benefits in relation to pensioner benefits since 2010.

With people on state pensions protected against inflation, it is hardly surprising that they should have benefited in relation to others. According to an IFS report in July 2016 analysing living standards, 'Median income for those aged 60 and over is now 11% above its 2007–08 level, for 31-59-year-olds it has returned to its 2007–08 level, but for 22-30-year-olds it is still 7% below'.[146] For anyone like Frank, Thomas or Mark who is well under 60 and has a learning disability, the impact of the government's courting of 'the grey vote' is obvious.

With working age benefits such as ESA frozen until 2020, inflation is likely to worsen the already precarious financial position of people like those in my case studies, particularly as the fall in the value of the pound since the referendum on EU membership in June 2016 is likely to lead to higher inflation.[147]

Whatever the rate of inflation, the most acute problem for someone like Danny is ensuring that he still gets his benefits. He is at the sharp end of the way the DWP has tightened its procedures but there are many more affected at every stage of the process.

In one example, a Capability for Work Questionnaire - twenty pages long and complicated for a relative or advocate to fill in - was sent in 2016 to Ian, someone who suffered brain damage in a car accident before reaching school age. Although his condition is not going to improve, he had twice in previous years attended a tribunal where on each occasion an initial decision to change his benefit status was overturned. Any system that was humane would not initiate the same process again in 2016.

That, of course, is precisely what the DWP did. As Ian has no back-up from family or support workers, if he had not had help from an advocate the form would not have been filled in, leading to a possible loss of or reduction in ESA – as the form itself spells out, 'we may stop the payments you already get'. The same sanction would have applied if he had not had an advocate either to accompany him to the subsequent Work Capability Assessment or to challenge the resulting decision to move him from the Support Group to the Work Related Activity Group[148], a change which meant a weekly reduction in his ESA of over £20.

These problems that can arise at each stage when someone lacks support of any kind should be easy to anticipate – but it seems they are not foreseen. The obvious conclusion to draw is that the procedures are intended to create a series of hurdles at each of which the DWP expects a percentage of those on benefits to fall – and either lose out financially or drop out of the system altogether. It is once more a reflection of the government's determination to save money, regardless of the needs of the disabled, their wellbeing and the facts of their circumstances.

An extreme instance of someone not just failing like Danny to clear the obstacles set by the DWP but dropping out of the system altogether is the experience of Alan, a 40 year old man with a background which should have triggered a sensitive response from any system that was fit for purpose. He was in foster care for eight years and between the ages of 10 and 18 attended a residential special school.

On reaching 18, in his opinion he was left by Social Services to fend for himself. He applied to join the army but was turned down on medical grounds because of a history of blackouts. From that point onwards, he was on benefits, receiving DLA and Income Support but with no back-up from family, support worker or advocate.

On 24 March 2016 he lost his Income Support. Because he didn't understand the procedure outlined in the accompanying letter, he missed the date by which a request for Mandatory Reconsideration had to be made. On 2 May, he was seen at home for approximately thirty minutes to discuss his PIP but was unclear who the person (presumably from the DWP) was and he didn't understand what was said to him. As a result, he lost his PIP, with a final payment being made on 27 May.

Without any support, he suffered in a way that Ian was able to avoid. From that final PIP payment in May 2016, he had no money on which to live for over seven months. During that period his only contact with the DWP was an unsuccessful interview for JSA at which, in his opinion, the staff dealing with him 'didn't give a shit'.

The interview, like the meeting on 2 May, is typical for Alan of the way he has been treated by many working for the DWP. He feels he has often been shown no respect, perhaps because staff had no experience of dealing with someone with a learning disability or because they had no training in using language that was clear for him.

From the end of May he went without either breakfast or lunch and only survived because of a friend who cooked one meal a day for him. He used his local food bank once, an experience that embarrassed him acutely – 'I felt like scum. I need money to buy my own food.' Because of Crohn's disease (which in his case means he has to avoid processed and high-fat foods) he had anyway to pass on what he was given there. He was also just able to stay in his flat where he has lived for two and a half years because his friend and his landlord withstood on his behalf the pressure to remove his housing benefit.

Later in the year, an advocacy organisation was contacted and steps were initiated to address his situation, as a result of which in January 2017 he had his ESA restored, a weekly payment of £73.10, the lower rate for someone in the Work Related Activity Group. Even this meagre sum, however, has since been reduced by a deduction of £14.80, a repayment charge to clear a debt of £2,091 resulting from overpayment of benefits in the past. He is therefore left with £58.30 a week, out of which he has to find £10 for electricity.

In May 2017, Citizens' Advice staff began the process of reactivating his PIP but at the time of going to print his total income was still less than £60 a week. While this is clearly better than the period of over seven months when he had to survive on nothing, it remains a paltry amount on which to scrape an existence.

The handling of Alan's case is made even worse by another element in his background: his younger brother, aged 36, committed suicide in 2015. With Alan's own record of depression, no system that was functioning effectively would put him through an extended period without any money when it posed an obvious risk to his mental health.

The inadequacies of mental health provision are another hazard for many like Alan, Danny and Ian. These problems have been highlighted repeatedly in the media in recent years and are shocking enough without the added complication of a learning disability. What makes the inadequacies worse is when they again appear to be driven by financial considerations, with such conditions as anxiety being seen as less significant than those experienced, in the words of George Freeman, Head of the government's No 10 Policy Unit, by 'really disabled people'[149].

This tactic of comparison ('x' is not as disabled as 'y') is used repeatedly by the government to drive down benefits for the disabled. It attempts to justify its measures by saying that its concern is to get help to those who most need it. For example, George Osborne, when interviewed by Channel 4 News in the run-up to the 2015 general election, refused to promise that there would no further cuts to disability benefits but would only say that the party would 'protect the most vulnerable'.

Theresa May used a similar justification on ITV's Facebook Live during the 2017 general election campaign after she had been tackled by a member of the public, Kathy Mohan, during a walkabout in Abingdon. On 15 May she told Robert Peston that disability benefit reforms were 'part of trying to ensure that we focus payments on those who most need it, those who are most vulnerable'. By that supposed 'logic', in the end there will just be one narrowly defined category of the disabled receiving benefits.

The individual is not being put at the heart of the way provision is planned – and not just in relation to mental health. Far too often the agencies involved are not doing what the Care Act recommends to ensure that 'conversations' about people's needs look at them holistically: 'local authorities and their partners must focus on joining up around an individual, making the person the starting point for planning, rather than what services are provided by what particular agency'.[150]

This failure to look at each individual holistically can be seen in all of my case studies. Austerity is not just creating isolated effects. As well as the decline in the value of their benefits and the reductions in support they have experienced in the austerity era - Frank from six hours to three, Les from six to five and Thomas from twelve to ten - there are many other elements in the cumulative impact of austerity: the loss of a befriender that Les suffered; reclassification of people in residential care as 'supported living' which means that someone like Les can no longer have access to a car; a change in the advocacy services available, partly because fewer referrals are now taken on an 'open door' basis[151] but also because of Council cuts despite the requirement under the Care Act for councils to fund advocacy services to which the learning disabled have access[152]; the loss of free art classes that Les had used; and the shrinking availability of social workers.[153]

Taken individually, each of the changes or cutbacks mentioned above is significant even though one or two may seem relatively minor; take them as a whole and their impact is profound, particularly when to all of these losses is added the decline in opportunities for the learning disabled to take up paid employment.

No-one in my case studies has had such employment, apart from Les before his early retirement, Mark as a teenager, Danny over twenty-six years ago and Frank in the equally distant past. His experience is typical of many: he has gone, over the years, from paid work to stable one day a week volunteering at local gardens – and finally to a financially unstable gardening project where funding is constantly under review. One factor in this trend in employment is the loss of the Council's Work Placement Officers, one of whom was instrumental in setting up Danny's day centre placement that he has kept for twenty-six years. Originally, there were five for the county; this declined to three (for West, Middle and East of the county); and now there are none, with Thomas's lost in approximately 2012.

The government would have us believe that these problems in getting employment are not happening. A DWP spokesman on 3 February 2017 made the following confident statement.[154]

'The number of disabled people in work has increased by almost 600,000 in the last three years, but we're determined to go even further.

'Our Work and Health Green Paper marks the next stage of our action to confront the attitudes, prejudices and misunderstandings that have become ingrained within the minds of employers and across wider society.

'Our welfare reforms are increasing the support and incentives for people to move into work, while keeping an important safety net in place for those who need it.

'In addition to ESA, we also offer support through Personal Independence Payments, to help with the extra costs associated with being disabled.'

Such pronouncements would sit nicely among the 'alternative facts' of the Trump administration. Who, however, would you rather believe, not just on employment statistics but on overall government strategy: the bland, seemingly soothing words of the DWP or the evidence of this book which reveals a supposed 'safety net' with gaping holes, some of them cut deliberately?

Life clearly wasn't blissful for someone with a learning disability before 2010 but the measures taken since then have drastically worsened the lives of many.

The years ahead will make matters worse. While there is the odd glimmer of hope from Theresa May's government – for example, the scrapping of retesting for chronically ill benefits claimants – she remains committed to the continuation of the previous government's austerity measures such as the working age benefits freeze.

Typical of what the future holds was a reduction from April 2017 in the rate of ESA for many by approximately £30.[155] The Work and Pensions Select Committee on 3 February 2017 had asked for this particular cut to be delayed. It found little evidence to support the view of the government, one that would not be out of place in a workhouse guardian in a Dickens novel, that lower payments would somehow motivate disabled people to find work.[156]

Such measures are a million miles from May's opening remarks on 13 July 2016 on becoming Prime Minister. Her 'mission' was 'to make Britain a country that works for everyone', phrasing that was to be picked up repeatedly in slogans at the Conservative Party Conference three months later: 'A party that works for everyone', 'A society that works for everyone', 'An economy that works for everyone'.

Her own speech at the Conference on 5 October 2016 built on the slogans. 'I want to set our party and our country on the path towards the new centre ground of British politics... built on the values of fairness and opportunity... where everyone plays by the same rules and where every single person regardless of their background, or that of their parents - is given the chance to be all they want to be... Government cannot stand aside when it sees social injustice and unfairness. If we want to make sure Britain is a country that works for everyone, government has to act to make sure opportunity is fairly shared... Because a society that works for everyone is a society based on fairness. And only genuine social reform can deliver it.'

The phrasing emerged again, through all the coughing, in her Conference speech the following year. Under the slogan of 'the British Dream' she pledged her determination to ensure 'our economy and society work for everyone in every part of this country, not just the privileged few'.

Her words seem like a clarion call for 'genuine social reform' and a commitment to 'fairness', with the concept repeated so many times in her words. And yet, of course, the apparent commitment bears no relation to reality, to the impact that austerity has had on people like Alan and Danny.

As long as it continues, for anyone with a learning disability such 'fairness' is a lie.

Postscript

The text of this book was completed in May 2017, some months before it appeared in print. Through the summer and autumn of 2017 and into 2018, life for the people with whom I volunteer continued to deteriorate.

Funding for the scheme that enabled Thomas to go surfing was withdrawn.

Cornwall Advocacy – one of the advocacy organisations referred to in Chapter 10 – was only saved from closure in December 2017 by a last-minute injection of funding from the Council. The support available to people with a learning disability remains precarious.

The most wide-ranging damage, however, was caused by the continuing 'roll-out' in Cornwall of Personal Independence Payments (PIP). Within the limited geographical area in which I work, two particularly shocking examples emerged.

One involved Michael who, like Alan, was left with no benefits whatsoever for a month because he failed to understand the letter informing him that he would not be transferred from DLA to PIP. The local food bank helped him survive for that period.

The second case concerned Jonathon, a man with diagnoses of autism and fibromyalgia and who had been reassessed by his social worker in July 2017 as needing additional support at home. Despite all this, in November 2017 he was not awarded PIP.

The impact of a PIP assessment was also felt by Frank, the focus of Chapter 4. In September 2017, he was not transferred from DLA to PIP. As a result his weekly income was cut from £158.70 to £115.10.

With many cuts still to come it seems inevitable that, by the time you are reading this, life for people with a learning disability will have deteriorated even further.

Footnotes

[1] Public Health England Learning Disabilities Observatory (2016), 'People with Learning Disabilities in England 2015' p.14.

[2] The Learning Disabilities Health Profile 2015 on the Public Health England website. At publication, more up-to-date figures were not available. A different number – over 1600 – for adults (18 to 64) with a learning disability getting long term support from the Local Authority was provided by Cornwall Council and is shown in Table 12 in Chapter 10.

[3] Many more adults with a learning disability are not picked up by the system, meaning that most figures are estimates. Local advocacy services work to a significantly higher figure than those given in the Learning Disabilities Health Profile 2015. 10,515 adults is the estimate for 2015 given by Cornwall Council itself in response to a Freedom of Information Request - Reference Number: IAR-101002881999. Different figures are given by Cornwall Council in Table 12 in Chapter 10 for the total number of adults (18-64) with a learning disability in Cornwall known to the local authority.

[4] 'Public perceptions of the adequacy of unemployment benefit levels have hardened over the past twenty years.' Baumberg, B. (2014), 'Benefits and the cost of living', British Social Attitudes: the 31st Report: NatCen Social Research p.96.

[5] For the disabled, language in the press had already deteriorated markedly in the previous decade. A report in 2011 entitled 'Bad News for Disabled People: How Newspapers are Reporting Disability', found among other trends, 'a significantly increased use of pejorative language to describe disabled people, including suggestions that life on incapacity benefit had become a lifestyle choice. The use of terms such as scrounger, cheat and skiver was found in 18% of tabloid articles in 2010/11 compared to 12% in 2004/5.' The research was conducted by the Strathclyde Centre for Disability Research and Glasgow Media Group, and commissioned by Inclusion London.

[6] IFS Post-Budget Briefing 2015 (9 July 2015) - Paul Johnson's opening remarks.

[7] Hood, A. (26 November 2015), IFS Presentation on Benefit and Tax Credit Changes. Presented at the IFS Post-Spending Review/Autumn Statement Analysis.

[8] Duffy, S. (2013), 'A Fair Society? How The Cuts Target Disabled People.' Published by the Centre for Welfare Reform on behalf of the Campaign for a Fair Society.

[9] House of Lords Select Committee on the Equality Act 2010 and Disability. Report of Session 2015–16. The Equality Act 2010: the impact on disabled people.
The phrase 'cumulative impact' was reiterated in the press release which accompanied the publication of 'Being Disabled in Britain: A Journey Less Equal', a comprehensive analysis published on 3 April 2017 by the Equality and Human Rights Commission: 'Social security reforms have had a particularly disproportionate, cumulative impact on the rights to independent living and an adequate standard of living for disabled people.'

[10] Adam,S. (17 March 2016), IFS Post-Budget Presentation on Personal Taxes and Benefits.

[11] The Resolution Foundation: Budget 2016 Response.

[12] Occasionally, however, such criticisms did seep out. In Cornwall, in 2011, Independent Wadebridge East councillor Mr Brewer told a charity worker, 'Disabled children cost the Council too much money and should be put down'. He re-told the Disability News Service (DNS) that he believed there was a good case for killing some disabled babies with high support needs because of the cost of providing them with the necessary services.

[13] For example, the introduction to British Social Attitudes; the 33rd Report: NatCen Social Research. Those same respondents in surveys who felt that the state was too generous to those on benefits did not feel the same when the benefit recipients became more specific. The researchers observed that while the public remained unsympathetic towards people without a job, especially those who don't have children, there was 'a reaction against cuts in the form of increased support for higher spending on benefits' for single parents and people who are disabled.

[14] Provisional data from ASHE (Annual Survey of Hours and Earnings 2016 Provisional Results): ONS licensed under the Open Government Licence v.3.0.

[15] Conversion carried out by using the Salary Calculator 2016-2017 - www.thesalarycalculator.co.uk.

[16] Provisional data from ASHE (Annual Survey of Hours and Earnings 2016 Provisional Results – see Regional Earnings section Table 8.1A). ONS licensed under the Open Government Licence v.3.0.

[17] Family Spending 2016. Table A1 – Components of Household Expenditure UK, financial year ending 2016. ONS licensed under the Open Government Licence v.3.0.

[18] The figures given by ONS and shown in the table (for example, 'Food and non-alcoholic drinks') total £529, not £528.90, presumably as a result of rounding up or down to a single decimal point.

[19] Excluding mortgage interest payments, Council Tax and Northern Ireland rates. Net rent is calculated as the amount spent after removing housing benefit, rebates and allowances received. Net rent makes up 44.83% of the total for 'Housing (net), fuel, power and water'.

[20] Charges for prescriptions (2.78%) and eye/dental treatment (12.5%) make up 15.28% of the total for 'Health'.

[21] Bus travel (excluding season tickets) makes up 0.96% of the total for 'Transport'.

[22] Mortgage interest payments and Council Tax make up 54.35% of the total for 'Other expenditure items'.

[23] Davis, A. Hill, K. Hirsch, D. and Padley, M. (2016), 'A Minimum Income Standard for the UK in 2016': Joseph Rowntree Foundation (JRF). Since 2008, JRF has published annual updates of the Minimum Income Standard (MIS) for the UK, to reflect changes in costs and living standards.

The definition of MIS that JRF works to is given on p.4 as follows: 'A minimum standard of living in the UK today includes, but is more than just, food, clothes and shelter. It is about having what you need in order to have the opportunities and choices necessary to participate in society … a minimum is about more than survival alone. However, it covers needs, not wants; necessities, not luxuries; items that the public think that people need in order to be part of society.'

This quotation and others later in the book have been reproduced by permission of the Joseph Rowntree Foundation.

[24] The categories used by the Joseph Rowntree Foundation (for example, 'Social and cultural participation') to arrive at a Minimum Income Standard are not identical to those used by the ONS. For that reason, only the total is given, with the rest of the column left blank.

[25] The adjustment has been made by using the data for the expenditure of a non-retired single person from Family Spending 2016 Table A23 - Expenditure by household composition UK, financial year ending 2016. ONS licensed under the Open Government Licence v.3.0.

All areas of expenditure (such as 'Food and non-alcoholic drinks') shown in my Table 1 have been reduced to the levels shown in ONS Table A23, with the exception of three 'non-essential' categories: 'Alcoholic drinks and tobacco', 'Recreation and culture' and 'Restaurants and hotels'. In these three categories, after the average expenditure of a non-retired single person of £308.50 has been deducted from UK full-time median net pay per week in April 2016 of £427, the money left over (£118.50) has been added proportionately to the levels shown in ONS Table A23.

[26] All areas of expenditure (such as 'Food and non-alcoholic drinks') shown in my Table 1 have been reduced to the levels shown in ONS Table A23, with the exception of three 'non-essential' categories: 'Alcoholic drinks and tobacco', 'Recreation and culture' and 'Restaurants and hotels'. In these three categories, after the average expenditure of a non-retired single person of £308.50 has been deducted from Cornwall full-time median net pay per week in April 2016 of £381, the money left over (£72.50) has been added proportionately to the levels shown in ONS Table A23.

[27] Although from my own experience this figure seems low, it is the correct average spending figure for an individual according to ONS Table A23.

[28] To help Frank - like Les and Thomas in later chapters - live independently, he receives support each week from Mencap under 'supported living' arrangements.

[29] This problem has been worsened by the introduction of PIP to replace DLA. For people with a long term health condition or disability, it has meant compulsory testing regardless of previous lifetime DLA. In one instance, reported in the Guardian on 14 September 2016, a thalidomide victim, Phil Spanswick, had his benefits cut because of the change.

The scrapping of retesting for chronically ill benefit claimants was announced by Damian Green, at that time Secretary of State for Work and Pensions, on 1 October 2016 but the detail on how this alteration in policy will be implemented has yet to emerge.

[30] This figure is made up of weekly payments for water, electricity and £5.63 towards his rent, the rest of which is covered by housing benefit. Maintenance and repairs are covered by the housing charity responsible for the flat. The amount he spent on water was previously much higher but has been reduced by the installation of a water meter. The overpayment is typical of the problems that someone like him can face: without a support worker, excessive charging for services can easily go undetected.

[31] This figure includes a regular weekly amount for cleaning materials etc. and an estimated average weekly amount for one-off purchases. He has had to buy all of his furniture and appliances himself, normally second-hand. In recent years, he has, however, bought a new washing machine because of the unreliability of his previous one, a new hoover and a new lawn mower.

[32] Apart from his buying non-prescription items such as plasters and painkillers, he has no spending in this area because he has free prescriptions. Dental treatment and eye tests are also free as long as his HC2 certificate is up-to-date.

[33] He lives within walking distance of some shops/services and, when needed, his support worker drives him to a supermarket or the surgery. He also has a bus pass for longer journeys. His annual bike service costs him an averaged weekly £1.10. The total also includes £12.40, the averaged weekly cost of his train fares to visit his parents and the Chelsea Flower Show.

[34] His spending in this area is relatively high because he has a landline and a mobile phone on a contract costing approximately £4.50 a week. He also spends a small amount on postage at Christmas.

[35] Apart from paying for his TV Licence, he regularly takes a local newspaper and sometimes buys a CD.

[36] He has an occasional Chinese takeaway or meal at Morrison's. An averaged weekly amount for food and other non-transport costs on his visit to the Chelsea Flower Show has also been included, with £1 added for presents bought for his family.

[37] He is exempt from paying Council Tax. He spends approximately £100 a year (averaged to produce a figure of £2 a week) on Christmas and birthday presents for his family. On top of this, he makes a regular donation to Cancer Research.

[38] In the table, his total spending is shown as £8.93 less than his income. He and his support worker found it difficult to account for where every last penny went but there is definitely no money saved at the end of each week.

[39] 54.35% of the total for 'Other expenditure items' in Table 2 – see footnote 22.

[40] Net rent makes up 44.83% of the total for 'Housing (net), fuel, power and water' in Table 2 – see footnote 19. Maintenance and repairs that for him are covered by the Council make up a further 10.48% of the total for 'Housing (net), fuel, power and water' in Table 2. His expenditure of £5.63 on rent has been added to the UK and Cornwall figures for 'Housing (net), fuel, power and water' columns of Table 4 to provide an accurate comparison with what he pays.

[41] In Table 2, charges for prescriptions and eye/dental treatment make up 15.28% of the total for 'Health' and bus travel (excluding season tickets which do not apply to any of my case studies) makes up 0.96% of the total for 'Transport' – see footnotes 20 and 21.

[42] The corresponding figures in the first two columns of Table 3 have been reduced by 55.31%, with his expenditure of £5.63 on rent added to produce a valid comparison – see footnote 40.

[43] The corresponding figures in the first two columns of Table 3, here and in subsequent chapters, unless stated otherwise, have been reduced by 15.28%.

[44] The corresponding figures in the first two columns of Table 3, here and in subsequent chapters, have been reduced by 0.96%.

[45] The corresponding figures in the first two columns of Table 3, here and in subsequent chapters, unless stated otherwise, have been reduced by 54.35%.

[46] As the categories used by the Joseph Rowntree Foundation to arrive at a Minimum Income Standard are not identical to those used by the ONS (see footnote 24), it was not possible to make the precise reductions for MIS specified for columns 1 and 2. Instead, the reduction of 15.62% in 'Spending on Cornwall full-time, median net pay per week April 2016' from £381 in Table 3 to £321.48 in Table 4 has been applied to the MIS total of £285 in Table 3. £5.63 has then been added – see footnote 40.

[47] It is hard to see why his HC2 certificate should need renewing as his circumstances are very unlikely to change.

[48] A scheme where someone who needs support and/or accommodation moves in with or regularly visits an approved Shared Lives carer, after they have been matched for compatibility.

[49] This figure is an estimate, derived from the £90 he takes out each week to live on and from the fact that he relies heavily on convenience food such as fish and chips. He could not be precise about how much was spent in this category.

[50] This average figure covers regular spending on clothing/footwear as well as one-off items such as his Somerset cricket shirts.

[51] All of his rent is covered by housing benefit. He also doesn't pay for maintenance and repairs. As a result, the corresponding figures in the first two columns of Table 2, here and in subsequent chapters, unless stated otherwise, have been reduced by 55.31% to produce a valid comparison.

[52] This figure is made up of weekly payments for water and electricity.

[53] This figure includes a regular weekly amount for cleaning materials etc. and an estimated average weekly amount for one-off purchases. Some furniture and appliances have either been bought second-hand or given or provided through a grant – for example, his cooker which is starting to show signs of unreliability and may soon need to be replaced. Other items – such as his television for which he had to save up – were new when bought.

[54] Apart from his buying non-prescription items such as plasters and painkillers, he has no spending in this area because he has free prescriptions. Dental treatment and eye tests are also free as long as his HC2 certificate is up-to-date.

[55] He lives within walking distance of most shops/services. He has a bus and a train pass. He uses the latter two or three times a year, for example when accompanied by a support worker to see Somerset play, for which average weekly expenditure is shown.

[56] He only has a landline. He also spends a small amount on postage at Christmas.

[57] This figure covers his TV Licence, weekly spending on DVDs and occasional spending on plants, model motorbikes and guides to plant care.

[58] The cost of the drawing tuition he received has not been included because it was after April 2016.

[59] His total of £13.50 includes an averaged weekly amount for food and other non-transport costs on his rare trips away. Pub lunches have also been included but not meals like fish and chips which are included in his regular food spending.

[60] He is exempt from paying Council Tax. He does, however, spend approximately £198 a year (averaged to produce a figure of £3.80 a week) on Christmas and birthday presents for his family.

[61] In the table, his total spending (once his weekly savings of £9.23 are included) is £5.64 less than his income. He and his support workers found it difficult to account for where every last penny went but there is definitely no further money saved at the end of each week.

[62] Under 'supported living' arrangements, each person has his or her own budget. The reclassification has the financial advantage for the Council of transferring accommodation costs to housing benefit, a central government responsibility.

[63] Before the 'supported living' arrangements took effect, when the car was used, it cost only 15p a mile. Now, if a support worker takes someone like Les out, it costs 43p a mile – an additional charge which he has to meet. A further consequence of the change to 'supported living' is that staff hours have been cut despite the fact that if taking the car is too expensive an option, more time is often needed to support individuals. For example, many at the residential home are not very mobile and to get to a hospital appointment without a car would need to use public transport. The residents have bus and/or train passes but the time taken on public transport uses up more staff hours and, of course, can be acutely uncomfortable for people with limited mobility.

[64] This precision in his memory extends to some other areas – he knows to the month how long he has been in his current flat and has achieved 100% in two assessments at the supermarket on food safety and hygiene – but not to everything, especially if it's further in the past. He will give me a lot of detail about changes in the work he is currently doing at the supermarket or the radio station but if I ask him about things he did as a child, very little detail is forthcoming, apart from occasional flashes of recollection like 'It was a sunny day like this when I went on the beach at Porthcawl'.

[65] He was initially allocated twelve hours in March 2013 when he was about to leave residential care but this was reduced later in the year to ten because his parents were deemed to be acting as his carers for two hours.

[66] The overall charge for support is reduced by Disability Related Expenditure (DRE) which takes into account spending needed as a result of an adult's disability. For Thomas, this includes costs like his front door exit sensor and components of his gas and electricity bills which arise from his requiring extra heating because of his disability.

[67] His spending in this area is lower than the average for the case studies because he has two subsidised main meals at the supermarket. He also has two or three meals a week provided by his parents.

[68] Some of his spending in this area, not included in the £10, comes from money he receives as Christmas presents.

[69] All of his rent is covered by housing benefit. He also doesn't pay for maintenance and repairs, apart from occasional replacement of small items such as a shower curtain. As a result, the corresponding figures in the first two columns of Table 2 have been reduced by 55.31%, with his expenditure of £1.00 on replacement of items added to produce a valid comparison.

[70] This figure is made up of weekly payments for water, gas and electricity, with an extra £1 added to cover the averaged cost of replacing minor items.

[71] This amount is for cleaning materials.

[72] He buys non-prescription items such as plasters and painkillers. Prescriptions, dental treatment and eye tests are free. He does, however, twice a year pay at a cost of £45 each time to see the dental hygienist because he doesn't always clean his teeth carefully enough. At the optician's, he chooses to pay for non-standard frames from a restricted range determined by the shape of his face. He also sees a chiropodist once every six weeks at a cost of £28 per visit – an average of £4.67 per week.

[73] He has a bus pass. To do his shopping, he is taken in his support worker's car and his other transport costs are covered by his parents taking him in their car.

[74] He has a landline and a mobile phone. He also spends a small amount on postage at Christmas.

[75] This figure covers his TV Licence, a lottery ticket, £5 a week given to his chapel collection, two magazines bought every week, games of pitch and putt and newspapers bought for their puzzles. Any spending on CDs is covered by money received as Christmas and birthday presents. The cost of his computer has not been included as it was bought by his parents.

[76] He has occasional meals out, normally in a supermarket – for example, if he goes out with his support worker or after pitch and putt. He also puts aside £60 each week to cover the cost of a holiday which is greatly inflated by his having to meet the expenses of a carer who accompanies him. This issue, which led to a protracted dispute with Cornwall Council, is explored in detail later in the chapter.

[77] This figure includes insurance cover for his washing machine, fridge-freezer and cooker. He also pays £6.19 a week for the exit sensor on his front door and a Lifeline panic button.

[78] He is exempt from paying Council Tax. He does, however, spend approximately £130 a year at Christmas and £60 on birthday presents for his family, averaged to produce a weekly figure of £3.65.

[79] To the total of £240.48 in Table 5, to provide a fair comparison £1 (for occasional replacement of items) has been added.

[80] The slight discrepancy between this figure (£189.98) and the amount he has left after paying towards the cost of his support (£190.24) arises because his parents could not account for every penny of his weekly spending.

[81] The total given in Table 6 is not used here because it falls £0.26 short of the amount he is left with each week to spend.

[82] See footnote 66.

[83] Davis, A. Hill, K. Hirsch, D. and Padley, M. (2016), 'A Minimum Income Standard for the UK in 2016' p.4: Joseph Rowntree Foundation.

[84] Davis, A. Hill, K. Hirsch, D. and Padley, M. (2016), 'A Minimum Income Standard for the UK in 2016' p.19: Joseph Rowntree Foundation.

[85] The Council had improved the chance of such a low turnout at the meeting by only sending an invitation to the individuals with a learning disability and not to their parents or carers. On other occasions, contact made by letter with Thomas, without a duplicate being sent to his parents, made life difficult for them. For example, if a letter arrived on a Tuesday, five days would already have elapsed by Sunday, the day on which Thomas, as part of his routine, takes letters around for his parents to see. The loss of five days made it much harder to meet a Council-imposed deadline.

[86] The same letter, because of the Council's failure to reply, has sometimes been sent as many as five times, with petrol costs added on for a journey from one Council office to another to ensure the appeal letter was delivered correctly and on time.

Obviously, frustration can be as big a factor here as cost. On a number of occasions, correspondence has not been answered without several reminders and phone calls have not been returned. For Thomas's father this reveals a lack of empathy and shows for him that the Council is not fit for purpose.

[87] See footnote 48.

[88] He is on the Sex Offenders Register because a 'mate' in prison used his Facebook 'wall' to make an inappropriate approach to an 11 year old girl. Mark is certain that he himself did nothing wrong but from the authorities' perspective, his being on the Register should have made them think twice before moving him into independent living.

[89] All of the categories left totally blank - 'Food and non-alcoholic drinks', 'Housing (net), fuel, power and water' and 'Household goods and services' – are ones where Laura's parents meet all of his costs. The totals in the columns for spending on UK and Cornwall median income have been reduced accordingly.

[90] He has high spending in this area. He estimates that he spends £36 a week on alcohol, most of it on Friday night and the remainder on Monday night. On top of that, he spends £2.50 refilling his e-cigarette which itself cost £17 – an averaged cost of £0.16 a week, assuming it lasts for two years.

[91] He has no spending in this area because he has free prescriptions. The cost of small non-prescription items such as plasters and painkillers is met by Laura's parents. Dental treatment and eye tests are also free as long as his HC2 certificate is up-to-date.

[92] His train fares from home to the centre cost £12.25 per five day week. Depreciation on his bike is approximately £100 a year or £2 a week. Over the year, he pays £10 for his Devon and Cornwall railcard and £42 for a new chain and tyre that are not covered by the bike's warranty – an extra £1 a week averaged over the year. He has no bus pass because he never uses buses and Laura's mother drives them both to darts matches at no cost to him.

[93] He has a pay-as-you-go mobile that, on average, costs him £10 a week. The phone itself – an old one of Laura's father's - has cost him nothing.

[94] His averaged weekly spending on PlayStation 3 computer games is £4.00. The cost of the TV Licence is covered by Laura's parents.

[95] The three-day darts trip to Somerset mentioned earlier costs £75 and only occurs once a year, giving an average weekly cost of £1.44. Laura's parents pay for occasional meals out.

[96] The cost of contents insurance is covered by Laura's parents.

[97] He spends approximately £80 on Christmas presents and £40 on a meal for Laura on her birthday, giving average weekly expenditure of £2.31. Council Tax is covered by Laura's parents.

[98] Because the spaces for 'Food and non-alcoholic drinks', 'Housing (net), fuel, power and water' and 'Household goods and services' have been left blank, the total for Minimum Income Standard has been adjusted. The reduction from the corresponding figure in Table 5 is 24.64%, the same as in the total given for Cornwall spending in the second column.

[99] The gap of £4.84 between his income and the expenditure shown above is made up by occasional weekday spending on food – sausage rolls, pasties etc.

[100] Spending by Laura's parents in certain categories such as 'Transport' makes a precise statistical comparison impossible.

[101] The term 'acquired brain injury' covers brain damage caused by events after birth, rather than as part of a genetic or congenital disorder.

[102] His period in hospital included time at a rehabilitation centre in Slough.

[103] For his gait, he has seen a podiatrist.

[104] He has regular appointments with a chiropractor to deal with this pain.

[105] The manager lets Danny remain at the centre without any funding from Social Services because he feels it would be an act of cruelty to remove what has been a key component of his life for twenty-six years. Admirable as this is on the manager's part, it is further evidence of a worrying trend where people like Danny attend a day centre without funding – and therefore with the financial strain passed from the Council to centre managers.

[106] Until 2008, he was visited at home at twelve month intervals to see if his condition had changed. At the last of those visits, his disability was defined as long term and not needing any further annual checks.

[107] In the Work Capability Assessment Handbook: for Healthcare Professionals (Gov.UK Guidance from DWP, updated 6 July 2016), there is nothing in the guidance (as the section below shows) to justify the restriction on how much Danny's mother was able to say.

'Section 3.1.3.3 Claimant accompanied by relative, friend, carer

'Claimants are encouraged to bring a friend or companion with them to the assessment, and feel more at ease if accompanied. Indeed the companion may be a prerequisite to enable them to come to the Assessment Centre.

'Companions will be able to give useful information, particularly in cases where the claimant has mental function problems, learning difficulties, cognitive problems or communication problems, or people who stoically understate their problems.

'In individuals with learning disability or cognitive impairment the role of the carer may be essential to establish their functional capabilities.'

65

[108] His optimism was only partly justified. When the result of the assessment came through, his ESA was taken away and he was moved onto JSA, giving him a smaller amount than he had previously received.

[109] Danny's low point score is typical of the outcome of many recent benefit assessments. The Guardian Online website on 17 April 2017 reported 'an apparent spike in people being turned down for Personal Independence Payment (PIP).

'Figures obtained by Angela Eagle, the former Work and Pensions minister, showed that 83,000 people assessed for their eligibility had been given zero scores for both components (daily living and mobility) in the six months between April and October 2016. That compares with 93,000 given a zero score for both components in the previous twelve months.'

[110] He did in fact go through everything that moving on to JSA entailed. With his mother and brother, on three consecutive days he went to his local Jobcentre office to register for the benefit. First, they were sent away to register online but that attempt failed because the system had no knowledge of his existence. Eventually, having part-filled in a booklet instead of doing it online, with the help of staff at the office he was registered for the new benefit.

[111] 'Mandatory reconsideration before appeal' was introduced for PIP and Universal Credit from April 2013 and, for other benefits, for decisions made on or after 28 October 2013. Before a claimant can appeal against a decision he or she has to ask for it to be looked at again by the DWP. Only once written notification of the result of the reconsideration is received can an appeal be lodged if the claimant is unhappy with the revised decision.

[112] According to data published on 16 March 2017 ('ESA: Outcomes of Work Capability Assessments including Mandatory Reconsiderations and Appeals: March 2017' at www.gov.uk/government/statistics), the figure of 59% for the quarter to December 2015 was in line with those over the previous two years.

[113] This unfairness was confirmed on 18 May 2017 in a report by Third Force News, published by the Scottish Council for Voluntary Organisations: 'A freedom of information (FOI) request revealed (DWP) staff are instructed via a key performance indicator to uphold 80% of decisions (at the Mandatory Reconsideration stage).' The same news report included comment from Phil Reynolds of Parkinson's UK: 'It is disgraceful that the DWP would use such arbitrary targets as a basis for decisions that have an enormous impact on the lives of people with long-term conditions, such as Parkinson's.'

[114] The precise amount someone receives as ESA can vary according to an individual's circumstances – hence the slight difference in the benefits received by Frank and Danny.

[115] An average of 50p a week covers the rare occasions that he goes to a pub.

[116] He doesn't pay for maintenance and repairs. He does, however, pay £7.33 towards his rent, the rest of which is covered by housing benefit. As a result, the corresponding figures in the first two columns of Table 2 have been reduced by 55.31%, with his expenditure on rent added to produce a valid comparison.

[117] This figure is made up of weekly payments for water, gas, electricity and rent.

[118] This figure includes a regular weekly amount for cleaning materials etc. and an estimated average weekly amount for one-off purchases such as his TV and washing machine. Carpets and several items of furniture (such as his microwave, sofa and chair) have been bought or passed on by his family.

[119] The corresponding figures in the first two columns of Table 3 have been reduced by 2.78% as only his prescriptions are free.

[120] Although he has free prescriptions, he does not have an HC2 certificate and therefore pays for dental treatment and visits to the optician. His dentist no longer does NHS work and an emergency extraction in 2016 (after Danny himself had tried to remove the tooth with a pair of pliers) cost £78. His nine-monthly check-up in the same year cost him £40 and a further £45 for a scale and polish. At the optician's, again in 2016, he paid for his eye test at £35, new frames at £59 and new lenses at £80 – with further possible spending of £80 on lenses for his spare glasses. He sees the chiropractor once every two months at an average weekly cost of £4.50. He also pays for non-prescription items such as plasters and painkillers.

[121] He has a bus pass. As, however, he aims to get into the centre as early as possible, he pays £2 each morning (Tuesday to Friday) for his bus ticket. Twice a week on average he completes his journey home from the centre by taxi – at a cost of £3 each time. In some weeks, he also needs to take a taxi to do his shopping, either each way or only one way, at a cost of £5 per journey. This has been averaged at a cost of £2 per week.

[122] He has a landline and a pay-as-you-go mobile on which he spends an average of £5 a month. The mobile phone itself cost him nothing. He also spends a small amount on postage at Christmas.

[123] This figure covers his TV Licence, his subscription for Sky TV and his buying the Star every day. He has also spent £6 on growbags this year. They only produced one tomato which someone stole but as he is going to try again, this is likely to be a recurring annual cost.

[124] This figure is for occasional family meals out.

[125] The corresponding figures in the first two columns of Table 2 have been reduced by 54.35%, with his expenditure of £7.47 on Council Tax added to produce a valid comparison.

[126] The figure includes his Council Tax and spending on presents. The family have agreed not to buy any for birthdays but at Christmas he spends approximately £140, averaged at £2.69 per week.

[127] To the total of £240.48 in Table 5, to provide a fair comparison £7.33 (on rent) and £7.47 (on Council Tax) have been added.

[128] In the table, his total spending is shown as £12.48 less than his income. He attributes this recent small 'surplus' to his giving up smoking.

[129] In all of the tables in this chapter, Mark has not been included because so many of his costs are met by his girlfriend's parents.

[130] See footnote 23.

[131] Care and Support Statutory Guidance Issued under the Care Act 2014 Department of Health October 2014 - p.7 section 1.2. Available at www.gov.uk/government/publications free of charge in any format or medium, under the terms of the Open Government Licence v.2.

[132] Care and Support Statutory Guidance Issued under the Care Act 2014 Department of Health October 2014 - p.7 section 1.4. Available at www.gov.uk/government/publications free of charge in any format or medium, under the terms of the Open Government Licence v.2.

[133] Care and Support Statutory Guidance Issued under the Care Act 2014 Department of Health October 2014 - p.10 section 1.17. Available at www.gov.uk/government/publications free of charge in any format or medium, under the terms of the Open Government Licence v.2.

[134] See footnote 23.

[135] Spending of those in the case studies is not compared in Tables 10 and 11 with the Minimum Income Standard because MIS is not broken down into categories like 'Recreation and culture' and 'Restaurants and hotels' – see footnote 24.

[136] 'Being Disabled in Britain: A Journey Less Equal', published in 2017 by the Equality and Human Rights Commission examined how the rights of disabled people (and not just those with a learning disability) are protected in Great Britain. It showed them as being 'left behind' and not just in a financial sense. The Commission's Chair, David Isaac, in an accompanying press release could not have been more trenchant: 'This report should be used as a call to arms. We cannot ignore that disabled people are being left behind and that some people – in particular those with mental health conditions and learning disabilities – experience even greater barriers.'

[137] See Chapter 4.

[138] In Cornwall in November 2014, the Council agreed the following cuts to adult care and support which, of course, includes care and support for people with learning disabilities: £2.7m in 2015-16; £3.5m in 2016-17; £4m in 2017-18; and £4.5m in 2018-19. The West Briton – 27 November 2014.

[139] Voyage Care is a UK-wide company that provides healthcare, social care and support.

[140] Learning Disability Voices comprises charities, not-for-profit and independent sector companies who provide learning disability services in the UK, including organisations such as Voyage Care, United Response, Lifeways, the Wilf Ward Family Trust, Hft and Mencap.

Learning Disability Voices exists, in its own words, 'to champion the learning disability sector and push for crucial policy changes to ensure a sustainable future for quality learning disability care'.

[141] Cannon was referring to social care in general but highlighted in the same article the fact that 'Today, support for people with learning disabilities comprises 30% of social-care funding.'

[142] Guardian Online - 13 July 2016. Article on Adult Social Care underfunding.

Later in the year, particularly in December 2016, the same paper's coverage was typical of the prominence given on television news bulletins and elsewhere in the press to Adult Social Care funding after the issue was not addressed in Philip Hammond's Autumn Statement.

Nonetheless, despite the arguments made – for example the LGA's calculation that councils in England and Wales between 2010 and 2015 had lost 350,000 full-time staff members – the government's response was inadequate. It gave councils 'freedom' to raise an additional 1% in Council Tax (on the adult social care precept) in each of the two following financial years, as long as the 'extra' money was recouped in the third. There was no real increase in funding and the appearance was given of responsibility resting with local councils.

Over the winter of 2016-17, however, pressure on the issue continued to mount and in his Budget on 8 March 2017 Philip Hammond announced that councils would receive an extra £2bn, spread over the next three years, to fund adult social care. The reaction of many was that the additional money would help if it came through to front-line services but that sustained investment rather than a short-term solution was needed.

[143] LGA press release - 31 January 2017.

[144] Freedom of Information Request Response - reference number: IAR-101003300436.

[145] The forms that appeared under the heading 'Payroll and Managed Account' are itemised below.

For Our Payroll Service

Monthly Payroll Service Application Form – 6 sides.

Authorising Your Agent Form – 2 sides.

Starter Checklist (for completion by your employees) – 2 copies, 1 side each.

Information Sheets – 3 sides.

For Our Managed Account Service

Authorisation form for payments to be made – 1 side.

Form for employee's bank account details for salary payment – 1 side.

[146] Belfield, C. Cribb, J. Hood, A. and Joyce, R. (2016), 'Living Standards, Poverty and Inequality in the UK: 2016': IFS.

[147] Emmerson, C. Hood, A. and Waters, T. (2016), 'Falling Sterling, Rising Prices and the Benefits Freeze': IFS. The authors noted that the 'sharp decline' in the value of the pound had affected significantly the likely rate of UK inflation. 'Just after the Budget, in its April World Economic Outlook, the International Monetary Fund (IMF) forecast CPI inflation to rise to 1.9% in 2017 before settling at 2.0% from 2018. By its October forecast the IMF had revised its inflation expectations to 2.5% in 2017 followed by 2.6% in 2018. Those forecasts were based on the exchange rate as it stood in mid-September; since then the pound has fallen a further 7% against the dollar and so, if anything, these numbers may in fact underestimate future price rises.'

[148] In the Work Related Activity Group he would have regular interviews with an adviser which is not the case in the Support Group.

[149] BBC News website - 26 February 2017.

The term 'really disabled people' was used by George Freeman in an interview with the BBC on 26 February 2017, after proposed changes to PIP. The changes were a response to two tribunal rulings at the end of 2016 which the government said would have added £3.7bn to the benefits bill by 2023.

In the interview Mr Freeman said: 'These tweaks are actually about rolling back some bizarre decisions by tribunals that now mean benefits are being given to people who are taking pills at home, who suffer from anxiety. We want to make sure we get the money to the really disabled people who need it.'

[150] Care and Support Statutory Guidance Issued under the Care Act 2014 Department of Health October 2014 - p.11 section 1.21. Available at www.gov.uk/government/publications free of charge in any format or medium, under the terms of the Open Government Licence v.2.

[151] A higher proportion of cases are now channelled through the Access Team, a body set up by Cornwall Council Adult Social Care. This procedure could create a conflict of interest if, for instance, a body established by Cornwall Council has to determine whether to approve a request for advocacy from someone whose principal grievance is the way he or she has been treated by Cornwall Council.

[152] Cornwall Advocacy has cut its service from three full-time advocates, each working 37.5 hours a week, to two, each of whom only works 15 hours a week, largely because of the removal of Cornwall Council funding that had been as high as £60,000 in previous years. Another advocacy organisation, Cornwall People First, has had its funding cut by 50% in the four years to April 2017.

[153] Thomas, as one example, has had no social worker since the end of 2014, apart from a brief period at the beginning of 2017. His parents feel that they have been doing the work that would formerly have been carried out by a social worker. When they have made this point to the Council, they have not been contradicted, a tacit admission that there is for most of the time no social worker available.

[154] BBC News Website - 3.2.17.

[155] New claimants of ESA who are placed in the Work Related Activity Group and new claimants in the Universal Credit Limited Capability for Work Group will receive the same rate as those claiming JSA.

[156] BBC News website – 3 February 2017.

Frank Field, the Committee chairman, was clear in his criticisms. 'We expect the government to respond to this report before the proposed new lower rate of ESA is due in April. If they intend to proceed with these cuts, we expect an explanation of how this will not be detrimental to its target of halving the disability employment gap, by making finding and keeping a job even more difficult for disabled people than it already is.'

Printed in Great Britain
by Amazon